Lumos Test Mastery
Grade 8 English Practice

ONLINE REGISTRATION REQUIRED

Visit the link below for online registration

lumoslearning.com/a/tedbooks

Access Code: TMG8ELA-63427-P

Why is Registration Mandatory?

 2 Lumos Diagnostic Tests

 Personalized Study Plan

 Automated Grading

 Answer Key & Explanations

INTRODUCTION

Lumos Test Mastery is an innovative blended test prep program that combines both print and online resources to help students excel in high-stakes state assessments and boost their grade-level skills.

The printed workbook features a wide variety of standards-aligned practice questions, giving students the opportunity to practice at their own pace and focus on the areas where they need the most help. These workbooks serve as invaluable tools for mastering critical state assessment skills, reinforcing concepts and abilities, bridging learning gaps, and much more.

Complementing this, the online program provides access to two comprehensive Lumos diagnostic tests that feature an array of technology-enhanced question types to meticulously evaluate student proficiency across essential standards. Based on the student's performance on the diagnostic tests, the online program crafts personalized study plans to deliver targeted remedial practice. Furthermore, the program grants access to an expansive question bank, enabling educators to craft their own questions and assessments that mirror the state tests.

Students can conveniently answer workbook questions using either printed or virtual bubble sheets, leading to swift, automated grading with instant feedback. This eliminates the need for manual grading of student responses, saving valuable time for parents and teachers.

Lumos Smart Test Prep Methodology

A Students take the first diagnostic test to evaluate their proficiency across essential standards.

B Based on their performance, the program creates a personalized study plan for targeted practice.

C Students complete the targeted remedial practice outlined in the study plan.

D Students take the second diagnostic test to gauge their mastery and progress.

E The program generates a second study plan, uncovering areas that demand further practice.

F Students complete the targeted practice to gain comprehensive mastery needed to ensure success on the state test.

How to Use the Lumos Program

GETTING STARTED

Parents & Caregivers: Register Online using the Access Code or by scanning the QR Code provided on the first page of this book. Select the *User Type as 'Student/Parent'* to get the login details for the Student and Parent Accounts in your registered email id.

Teachers: Register Online using the Access Code or by scanning the QR Code provided on the first page of this book. Select the *User Type as Teacher* to get the login details for the Teacher Account in your registered email id. Using the *My Student* option on the menu, add a student. Provide the login details to your student for online access. Please note that access for 1 student is included in the program. For additional student licenses and school purchases, contact us at **support@lumoslearning.com**

TAKING THE DIAGNOSTIC TEST: Login to the student account. Click on the *Bell Icon* on the top right-hand corner or *Start Test* button on the home page. The test is also available on the table of contents in the student account.

GETTING THE STUDY PLAN: On completing the diagnostic test, a personalized study plan is generated which outlines the lessons to be practiced in this printed workbook. To access the study plan, click on the *STUDY PLAN* button on the online table of contents. The student must complete the study plan by practicing the lessons in this workbook.

COMPLETING LESSONS IN THIS WORKBOOK: Using the table of contents in this book, goto the lessons mentioned in the study plan. You will find a *Printed Bubble Sheet* before every lesson which may be used by the student to answer the questions. Instructions on *How to Use the Printed Bubble Sheet* are provided at the end of this book. Alternatively, the student may also answer the questions using the *Virtual Bubble Sheet* in the student account.

GRADING ANSWERS: On submitting the answers, the progam uses the *Automated Grading* feature to get the results. For grading open-ended questions, login to your parent/teacher account and grade them manually.

ANSWERS & EXPLANATIONS: Answers and detailed explanations are provided in the student results page. You can also login to your parent/teacher account and click on the *Preview* icon under *My Lessons* to view the answer explanations.

MONITORING STUDENT PROGRESS: You can view the performance reports of the student in the *Reports* section of the parent/teacher account.

COMPLETING THE PROGRAM: After completing the first study plan, take the second diagnostic test. Finish the study plan before the actual state test.

Table of Contents

Chapter 1
Reading Literature

Test ID	8E001
Test Name	**Textual Evidence**
Student Name	
Date	

1	Ⓐ Ⓑ Ⓒ Ⓓ	**6**	Ⓐ Ⓑ Ⓒ Ⓓ	**10 B**	Ⓐ Ⓑ Ⓒ Ⓓ
2	Ⓐ Ⓑ Ⓒ Ⓓ	**7**	Ⓐ Ⓑ Ⓒ Ⓓ	**11 A**	Ⓐ Ⓑ Ⓒ Ⓓ
3	Ⓐ Ⓑ Ⓒ Ⓓ	**8**	Ⓐ Ⓑ Ⓒ Ⓓ	**11 B**	Ⓐ Ⓑ Ⓒ Ⓓ
4	Ⓐ Ⓑ Ⓒ Ⓓ	**9**	Ⓐ Ⓑ Ⓒ Ⓓ	**12 A**	Ⓐ Ⓑ Ⓒ Ⓓ
5	Ⓐ Ⓑ Ⓒ Ⓓ	**10 A**	Ⓐ Ⓑ Ⓒ Ⓓ	**12 B**	Ⓐ Ⓑ Ⓒ Ⓓ

Lesson 1: Textual Evidence

Question 1-5 are based on the poem below

Sympathy

I lay in sorrow, deep distressed;
My grief a proud man heard;
His looks were cold, he gave me gold,
But not a kindly word.

My sorrow passed-I paid him back
The gold he gave to me;
Then stood erect and spoke my thanks
And blessed his charity.

I lay in want, and grief, and pain;
A poor man passed my way;
He bound my head, He gave me bread,
He watched me day and night.

How shall I pay him back again
For all he did to me ?
Oh, gold is great, but greater far
Is heavenly sympathy.
-        Charles Mackay

1. The reader can tell from the third stanza that the poet is

Ⓐ   caring for a patient with a head injury.
Ⓑ   wanting company.
Ⓒ   watched and fed night and day by a poor man.
Ⓓ   greedy.

2. According to the poet, what did he feel was most important?

Ⓐ   giving away food
Ⓑ   blessing charity
Ⓒ   sympathy
Ⓓ   gold

3. What does the first stanza tell us about the poet?

Ⓐ   The poet experienced an event which made him deeply sorrowful.
Ⓑ   The poet wrote this poem when he was a proud man.
Ⓒ   The poet wrote this poem when he was in need of money.
Ⓓ   The poet was friends with the proud man.

4. Which line in the poem tells you that the poet is grateful to the poor man?

Ⓐ How shall I pay him back again, for all he did to me?
Ⓑ I lay in want, in grief and pain;
Ⓒ His looks were cold, he gave me gold. But not a kindly word.
Ⓓ Then stood erect and spoke my thanks, and blessed his charity.

5. How did the proud man treat the poet when he lay in sorrow and deep distress?

Ⓐ in an affectionate way
Ⓑ in an aloof, unsympathetic manner
Ⓒ with a lot of concern
Ⓓ with respect and kindness

Question 6 and 7 are based on the poem below

The Mountain and The Squirrel	The Arrow and the Song
The mountain and the squirrel Had a quarrel; And the former called the latter, "Little Prig." Bun replied "You are doubtless very big; But all sorts of things and weather Must be taken in together To make up a year And a sphere. And I think it no disgrace To occupy my place. If I'm not so large as you, Your are not so small as I, And not half so spry; I'll not deny you make A very pretty squirrel track; Talents differ; all is well and wisely put; If I cannot carry forests on my back, Neither can you crack a nut" Ralph Waldo Emerson (1803 - 1882)	I shot an arrow into the air It fell to earth, I knew not where; For, so swiftly it flew, the sight Could not follow it in its flight. I breathed a song into the air It fell to earth, I knew not where For who has sight so keen and strong That it can follow the flight of song? Long, long afterward, in an oak I found the arrow, still unbroke And the song, from beginning to end I found again in the heart of a friend. H. W. Longfellow (1807 - 1882)

6. **Which line in "The Mountain and the Squirrel" told the reader that the squirrel recognizes everyone has a different talent?**

 Ⓐ Talents differ; all is well and wisely put;
 Ⓑ You are doubtless very big;
 Ⓒ And I think it no disgrace
   To occupy my place.
 Ⓓ I'll not deny you make
   A very pretty squirrel track;

7. **Which of the following statements about "The Mountain and the Squirrel" and "The Arrow and the Song" is true?**

 Ⓐ A squirrel is the narrator in both.
 Ⓑ Both incorporate nature in the text.
 Ⓒ Both are written in first person.
 Ⓓ Both are about friendship.

Question 8-10 are based on the poem below

The Lake Isle of Innisfree

I will arise and go now, and go to Innisfree,
And a small cabin build there, of clay and wattles made:
Nine bean-rows will I have there, a hive for the honey-bee;
And live alone in the bee-loud glade.

And I shall have some peace there, for peace comes dropping slow,
Dropping from the veils of the morning to where the cricket sings;
There midnight's all a glimmer, and noon a purple glow,
And evening full of the linnet's wings.

I will arise and go now, for always night and day
I hear lake water lapping with low sounds by the shore;
While I stand on the roadway, or on the pavements grey,
I hear it in the deep heart's core.

W.B. Yeats

About the poet:
William Butler Yeats was an Irish poet and a dramatist. He was one of the foremost figures of 20th-century literature and was the driving force behind the Irish literary revival. Together with Lady Gregory and Edward Martin, Yeats founded the Abbey Theatre. He served as its chief during its early years and was a pillar of the Irish literary establishment in his later years.

The well-known poem explores the poet's longing for the peace and tranquillity of Innisfree, a place where he spent a lot of time as a boy. This poem is a lyric.

image obtained from freephotosbank.com

8. Which line tells the reader Yeats is day-dreaming of Innisfree?

Ⓐ Nine bean-rows will I have there, a hive for the honey-bee;
Ⓑ And I shall have some peace there, for peace comes dropping slow,
Ⓒ And evening full of the linnet's wings.
Ⓓ While I stand on the roadway, or on the pavements grey

9. What does the description after the poem tell us about Yeats?

Ⓐ He was a key person in the development of Irish economy.
Ⓑ He was a key person in the development of Irish literacy.
Ⓒ He was not a Nobel Prize winner.
Ⓓ all of the above

10. Part A

According to the poem and the description, which of the following statements about the author would be true?

Ⓐ Yeats was very famous and loved literature.
Ⓑ Yeats was a writer and wrote a lot of poems and plays.
Ⓒ Yeats was an Irish man and a key person in the development of Irish literature.
Ⓓ All of the above.

10. Part B

Which line of the poem provides evidence that the author wants to build a cabin in Innisfree?

Ⓐ I will arise and go now, and go to Innisfree,
Ⓑ And a small cabin build there, of clay and wattles made:
Ⓒ Dropping from the veils of the morning to where the cricket sings;
Ⓓ I will arise and go now, for always night and day

Question 11 is based on the passage below

Patrick couldn't believe it. The most important day of his life so far; the day he had been waiting for had finally arrived! He was so excited to show the coaches how hard he had been working on his pitching. He just knew he would make the team this year. Looking at the clock, Patrick realized he was running late. "Bye, Mom," he yelled as he scrambled out of the house. Backing down the driveway, he saw his mom run out of the house, and it looked like she was trying to get his attention. He didn't have time to wait, so he drove off.

Although the school was only five minutes away, the drive felt like an eternity. Two red lights later, Patrick screeched into the parking lot, slammed the car into park, and ran around to the trunk to get his bat bag. It wasn't there. Every piece of equipment he needed to prove himself to the coaches this year was in that bag.

11. Part A

What was Patrick's mom likely trying to tell him?

Ⓐ "Don't drive too fast!"
Ⓑ "Don't be late for tryouts!"
Ⓒ "Be careful driving!"
Ⓓ He forgot his bat bag!

11. Part B

The reader can tell from the story that Patrick _____.

Ⓐ had tried out for the team before and not made it.
Ⓑ was a fast runner.
Ⓒ was not at all ready for tryouts.
Ⓓ was not excited to tryout for the team.

Question 12 is based on the passage below

It had been a year since Lauren had seen Bailey. Bailey's family had moved to Qatar leaving Lauren to face the world without her best friend. Anxiously, Lauren waited at the arrival gate hoping to glimpse a peek at her childhood friend. She knew after eleven hours in the air, Bailey would be exhausted, but she could hardly wait to catch up. Moments later, the doors to the gate flung open, and there she was, her best friend, Bailey.

Once home, the hours passed like minutes as the girls laughed and giggled sharing moments from the last year. It felt as if they had never been apart. But Lauren felt like Bailey was holding something back.

12. Part A

What details in the passage supports that Lauren was anxious to meet her friend Bailey?

Ⓐ She knew after eleven hours in the air, Bailey would be exhausted, but she could hardly wait to catch up.

Ⓑ Anxiously, Lauren waited at the arrival gate hoping to glimpse a peek at her childhood friend.

Ⓒ Moments later, the doors to the gate flung open and there she was, her best friend, Bailey.

Ⓓ All of the above

12. Part B

What did Lauren feel about Bailey in the concluding sentence of the passage?

Ⓐ Bailey was moving home.

Ⓑ Bailey had a secret she wasn't sharing.

Ⓒ Bailey loved her new home in Qatar.

Ⓓ None of the above

Test ID	8E002
Test Name	Inferences
Student Name	
Date	

1	Ⓐ Ⓑ Ⓒ Ⓓ	6	Ⓐ Ⓑ Ⓒ Ⓓ	10 B	Ⓐ Ⓑ Ⓒ Ⓓ
2	Ⓐ Ⓑ Ⓒ Ⓓ	7	Ⓐ Ⓑ Ⓒ Ⓓ	11	Ⓐ Ⓑ Ⓒ Ⓓ
3	Ⓐ Ⓑ Ⓒ Ⓓ	8	Ⓐ Ⓑ Ⓒ Ⓓ	12	Answer in the space provided below.
4	Ⓐ Ⓑ Ⓒ Ⓓ	9	Ⓐ Ⓑ Ⓒ Ⓓ	13	Ⓐ Ⓑ Ⓒ Ⓓ
5	Ⓐ Ⓑ Ⓒ Ⓓ	10 A	Ⓐ Ⓑ Ⓒ Ⓓ		

12

Chapter 1 → Lesson 2: Inferences

Question 1 and 2 are based on the poem below

The Lake Isle of Innisfree

I will arise and go now, and go to Innisfree,
And a small cabin build there, of clay and wattles made:
Nine bean-rows will I have there, a hive for the honey-bee;
And live alone in the bee-loud glade.

And I shall have some peace there, for peace comes dropping slow,
Dropping from the veils of the morning to where the cricket sings;
There midnight's all a glimmer, and noon a purple glow,
And evening full of the linnet's wings.

I will arise and go now, for always night and day
I hear lake water lapping with low sounds by the shore;
While I stand on the roadway, or on the pavements grey,
I hear it in the deep heart's core.

W.B. Yeats

About the poet:
William Butler Yeats was an Irish poet and a dramatist. He was one of the foremost figures of 20th-century literature and was the driving force behind the Irish literary revival. Together with Lady Gregory and Edward Martin, Yeats founded the Abbey Theatre. He served as its chief during its early years and was a pillar of the Irish literary establishment in his later years.

The above well-known poem explores the poet's longing for the peace and tranquility of Innisfree, a place where he spent a lot of time as a boy. This poem is a lyric.

1. After reading the poem what can you say the poet is yearning for?

Ⓐ the lake water and the sound it makes
Ⓑ the beehive and sound of the bees
Ⓒ the peace and tranquility of Innisfree
Ⓓ none of the above

2. According to the poem, what do you think the age of the author is?

Ⓐ He is old and ready to retire.
Ⓑ He is a very young boy.
Ⓒ He is in his mid thirties.
Ⓓ He is a baby.

Question 3 is based on the paragraph below

Elizabeth had done it again. She was in such a hurry; she didn't check to make sure she had everything she needed for the drive to work. Just as she slammed the door behind her, she realized, too late, that she wasn't going anywhere fast.

3. What did Elizabeth forget?

- Ⓐ her running shoes
- Ⓑ her keys
- Ⓒ her briefcase
- Ⓓ her workout clothes

Question 4 is based on the paragraph below

When Samantha saw the new boy in class, her heart started pounding so fast and loudly that she was certain everybody could hear it. She straightened her posture and gently swept her bangs behind her right ear. As the boy sat down next to her, she gave him a quick glance and then a friendly smile. She was sure he noticed her bright red cheeks as she bent over her paper.

4. Which of the following can be inferred about Samantha based on the above passage?

- Ⓐ She thought the boy had a nice backpack.
- Ⓑ She was scared of the boy.
- Ⓒ She thought the boy was cute.
- Ⓓ She thought the boy was mean.

Question 5 is based on the paragraph below

Maya and her family were headed to the beach one sunny summer afternoon. When they arrived, Maya noticed a family seemed to be having what appeared to be a garage sale, which was a curious sight to see in the beach parking lot. They were selling used personal items that you would normally find in one's house like pots, pans, dishes, a CD player, and various other items. There appeared to be a mother, father, and two children, a boy and a girl about Maya's age. Maya could tell that the family was not there to enjoy the beach as they were not dressed for the beach. Their clothes were far too warm for the beautiful day and were tattered, torn, and quite dingy. Suddenly, Maya remembered that she had a twenty dollar bill in her pocket that she had received for her birthday.

5. Based on the information in the passage, infer what you think will happen next.

- Ⓐ Maya will buy something from the family's garage sale.
- Ⓑ Maya will want to buy something, but she already has all of those items in her house, so she won't buy anything.
- Ⓒ Maya will give the money to her family.
- Ⓓ Maya will use the money for snacks for the family.

After reading the story, enter the details in the map below. This will help you to answer the questions that follow.

Haley was putting the finishing touches on her famous apple pie when the phone rang. She dashed to answer it. After all, this might be the call that she had been waiting for. Even though her hands were still covered in flour, she grabbed the phone before it could ring a second time.

"Hello. You've reached the Williams residence," she said, trying to make her voice sound calm and collected.

"Is this Haley Williams?" asked the voice on the other end of the line.

"Yes, it is. How may I help you?" Haley replied.

"Ms. Haley Williams, we are proud to announce that you are a finalist in the National Pie Competition. The championship round will be held next weekend in Tampa, Florida. You and your family are invited to join us. Good luck!"

"Why thank you very much," Haley said graciously. "I am looking forward to it." After hanging up, Haley took a deep breath and let out an ear-piercing scream of excitement. She jumped up and down and ran around the kitchen with glee. In the pandemonium, her apple pie was knocked off the counter and landed on the floor, where her two puppies immediately began to gobble it down. Haley just laughed at the mess. As she cleaned the floor she began to think very carefully about her plan for the upcoming week.

With the big competition only one week away, Haley decided that she better make three pies every day. This practice would allow her to experiment with the crust , the filling, and the baking time. She wanted to do everything she possibly could to ensure that her pie was a winner.

Her friend, Max, who was thrilled to find out that Haley was a finalist, offered his kitchen for practice. Haley thanked him. She knew that cooking in an unfamiliar kitchen would be excellent practice for the competition.

Haley worked hard all week, doing nothing but baking pies. Not every pie turned out well. Some had a soggy crust or burned a little on the top. Haley threw out the bad pies and carefully wrapped the successful pies and delivered them to her neighbors and friends. They were all delighted by the surprise and wished Haley good luck at the competition.

The day before the competition, Haley packed up all of the things she would need. She brought her favorite rolling pin for good luck. When she arrived in Tampa, Florida, she went straight to her hotel and got a good night's rest. The competition started early the next morning, and Haley wanted to be ready.

The day of the competition seemed to fly by in one big blur. Haley was one of twelve finalists. Each finalist had their own counter top on which to prepare their pie and their own oven in which to bake it. Once everyone was set up at their station, the master of ceremonies officially started the clock, and everyone got to work. Every contestant had 90 minutes to prepare and bake their pies. Haley mixed and rolled out her pie dough. Then she peeled and sliced her apples, laying them carefully inside the crust. She seasoned the pie with cinnamon and sugar and laid strips of dough on top. She brushed the pie crust with butter and glanced at the clock. She was right on schedule; her pie took 45 minutes to bake and there were just 47 minutes left on the clock.

Haley opened the oven door, but she immediately noticed that something was wrong.

She didn't feel a rush of dry heat in her face, and she realized that she had forgotten to preheat the oven. The oven wasn't hot, and it would take several minutes to reach the correct temperature.

Haley felt her heart sink into her stomach. How could she forget such an important step? In all her practice, she had never forgotten to preheat the oven. Haley figured that she didn't stand a chance of winning, but she refused to give up. She put her pie in the oven and set the oven to the correct temperature.

With 30 seconds left in the competition, Haley removed her pie from the oven. It wasn't golden on the top, but it looked like it was cooked through. Haley sighed, disappointed that she had blown her chances at winning. But she delivered her pie to the judges and hoped for the best.

After tasting each pie and deliberating for hours, the judges handed the results to the master of ceremonies. "In third place….Haley Williams!" the voice boomed over the loud speaker. Haley couldn't believe her ears. She walked to the front of the room to accept her trophy with a smile on her face. She knew that if it hadn't been for her mistake, she might have won the grand prize.

But, she just hugged her trophy, congratulated herself on her accomplishment, and promised herself that she would do better next year.

Title

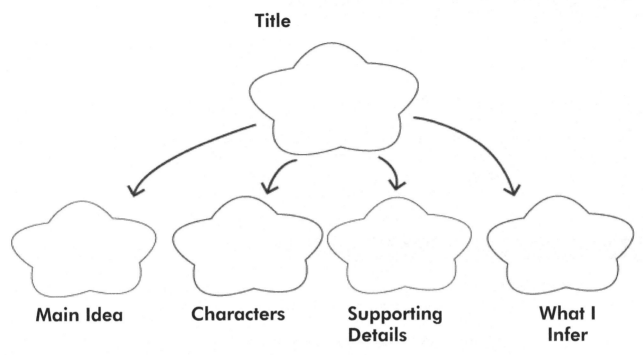

Main Idea   Characters   Supporting   What I
                                       Details   Infer

6. What can be inferred from Haley's reaction to the phone ringing?

Ⓐ She isn't concerned about the phone call.
Ⓑ She doesn't think washing her hands is important.
Ⓒ She is expecting an important phone call.
Ⓓ She is enjoying talking to her family.

Question 7 is based on the paragraph below

Henry sat eagerly in the waiting area of the airport. Over the last year, he'd been putting away a little money each month into what he called his "vacation fund." He bought travel books and researched all of the sites he wanted to see. Now all he had to do was wait until his flight was called.

7. What can you infer about Henry's trip?

Ⓐ It was a spur of the moment idea.
Ⓑ It is something he has looked forward to for a long time.
Ⓒ It is to a place he's been before.
Ⓓ It is to an exotic location.

Question 8 is based on the paragraph below

She pulled hard at the doorknob. The door was difficult to budge. Finally inside, she brushed aside the cobwebs, leaving footprints in the dust on the floor.

8. What can be inferred from this description?

- Ⓐ The place she is entering hasn't been used in a long time.
- Ⓑ The house she is entering is a new structure.
- Ⓒ The door was locked.
- Ⓓ She has just bought the house and is preparing to move in.

Question 9 is based on the paragraph below

When Melody's mom came home and discovered the vase in pieces on the counter, she said nothing; instead she pursed her lips, put her hand on her left hip and glared at Melody.

9. What can the reader infer about Melody's mom?

- Ⓐ Melody's mom is mad at Melody for breaking the vase. She is waiting for an explanation.
- Ⓑ Melody's mom had a long day at work and just needs a moment to think.
- Ⓒ Melody's mom cannot talk due to some dental work she had done earlier in the day.
- Ⓓ Melody's mom is surprised that her kitchen is so clean.

Question 10 is based on the poems below

The Mountain and The Squirrel	The Arrow and the Song
The mountain and the squirrel Had a quarrel: And the former called the latter, "Little Prig." Bun replied, "You are doubtless very big: But all sorts of things and weather Must be taken in together To make up a year And a sphere. And I think it no disgrace To occupy my place. If I'm not so large as you You are not so small as I, And not half so spry; I'll not deny you make A very pretty squirrel track; Talents differ; all is well and wisely Put; If I cannot carry forests on my back, Neither can you crack a nut." **RALPH WALDO EMERSON (1803 -1882)**	I shot an arrow into the air It fell to earth, I knew not where: For, so swiftly it flew, the sight Could not follow it in its flight. I breathed a song into the air It fell to earth, I knew not where For who has sight so keen and strong That it can follow the flight of song? Long, long afterward, in an oak I found the arrow, still unbroke And the song, from beginning to end I found again in the heart of a friend. **H.W. LONGFELLOW (1807 -1882)**

10. Part A

What do you think the poet is trying to tell us in the "The Arrow and the Song"?

Ⓐ Actions and words can leave a lasting impact on others.
Ⓑ It is dangerous to shoot arrows into the air.
Ⓒ Arrows shot into the air sound like a beautiful song.
Ⓓ None of the above

Part B

What do you think is the poet trying to tell us in both poems?

Ⓐ What goes around comes around.
Ⓑ The actions we perform or the thoughts we express will leave their mark.
Ⓒ We must think before we do our actions.
Ⓓ The arrow and the song both fell to the ground.

11. When the thunder began to roar, Mary leapt under her covers and put her hands over her ears.

   What can be inferred from Mary's reaction to the storm?

   Ⓐ She enjoys thunderstorms.
   Ⓑ She cannot hear well.
   Ⓒ She is afraid of thunderstorms.
   Ⓓ She likes to sleep.

Question 12 is based on the paragraph below

She pulled hard at the doorknob. The door was difficult to budge. Finally inside, she brushed aside the cobwebs, leaving footprints in the dust on the floor.

12. What can be inferred from this description?

Question 13 is based on the paragraph below

Justin had Mark's deep brown eyes and his button nose. At only three years old, he already showed signs of Mark's sense of humor and optimism. Mark was proud that Justin had inherited some of his traits.

13. Based on the description above, one could infer that Justin _____

   Select the correct answer choice from the 4 options given below and fill in the blank.

   Ⓐ   is friends with Mark
   Ⓑ   is Mark's brother
   Ⓒ   is Mark's son
   Ⓓ   is Mark's sister

Test ID	8E003
Test Name	Theme
Student Name	
Date	

1	Ⓐ Ⓑ Ⓒ Ⓓ	6	Ⓐ Ⓑ Ⓒ Ⓓ	10	Ⓐ Ⓑ Ⓒ Ⓓ
2	Ⓐ Ⓑ Ⓒ Ⓓ	7 A	Ⓐ Ⓑ Ⓒ Ⓓ		
3	Ⓐ Ⓑ Ⓒ Ⓓ	7 B	Ⓐ Ⓑ Ⓒ Ⓓ		
4	Ⓐ Ⓑ Ⓒ Ⓓ	8	Ⓐ Ⓑ Ⓒ Ⓓ		
5	Ⓐ Ⓑ Ⓒ Ⓓ	9	Ⓐ Ⓑ Ⓒ Ⓓ		

Chapter 1 → Lesson 3: Theme

1. What is the difference between a theme and a main idea?

    (A)   A theme is the message of a story, and the main idea is what the story is about.
    (B)   A theme is a summary, and the main idea is a paraphrase.
    (C)   A theme tells what the symbols mean, and the main idea is a symbol.
    (D)   A theme is what a student writes, and a main idea is what the story is mainly about.

2. What is a universal theme?

    (A)   a story that takes place in outer space
    (B)   a theme that is implied
    (C)   a common theme that could apply to anyone, anywhere, anytime
    (D)   a theme that includes an adventure across the universe

3. The theme of a story:

    (A)   is always a statement.
    (B)   is usually a single word, such as "love."
    (C)   is a question.
    (D)   none of the above.

4. What is the best way to find a theme in a story?

    (A)   look at the first sentence of the story.
    (B)   look at the names of the characters in a story.
    (C)   look at the details in the story to find a larger meaning.
    (D)   look at reviews of the story.

5. What is an implied theme?

    (A)   a theme that is straightforward and requires no guessing
    (B)   a theme that is indirectly stated through characters, plot, and setting of a story
    (C)   a theme that is common throughout many stories that are told across many different cultures
    (D)   a theme that is clearly stated by the main character in the story

After reading the story, enter the details in the map below. This will help you to answer the questions that follow.

The Fox and the Cat - An Aesop's Fable

A Fox was boasting to a Cat of its clever devices for escaping its enemies.
"I have a whole bag of tricks," he said, "which contains a hundred ways of escaping my enemies."
"I have only one," said the Cat; "but I can generally manage with that."
Just at that moment they heard the cry of a pack of hounds coming towards them, and the Cat immediately scampered up a tree and hid herself in the boughs.
"This is my plan," said the Cat. "What are you going to do?"

The Fox thought first of one way, then of another, and while he was debating the hounds came nearer and nearer, and at last the Fox in his confusion was caught up by the hounds and soon killed by the huntsmen. The Cat, who had been looking on, said, "Better one safe way than a hundred on which you cannot reckon."

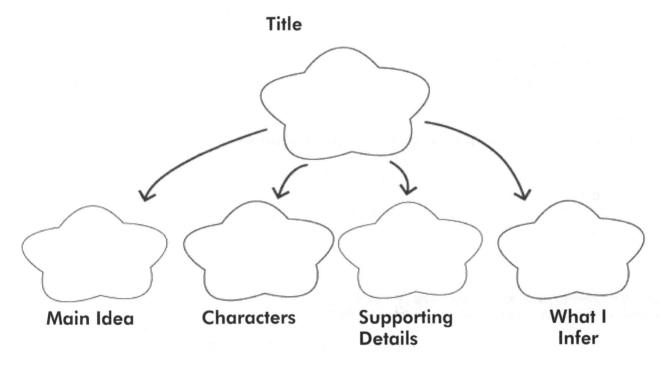

6. What is the theme of this story?

Ⓐ   It is good to make friends with strangers.
Ⓑ   It is better to be a cat than a fox.
Ⓒ   Having one solid plan is better than having many possible ones.
Ⓓ   Foxes are not as smart as cats.

The Ungrateful Son
by Jacob and Wilhelm Grimm

Once, a man was sitting with his wife before their front door. They had a roasted chicken, which they were about to eat together. Then the man saw that his aged father was approaching, and he hastily took the chicken and hid it, for he did not want to share it with him. The old man came, had a drink, and went away. Now the son wanted to put the roasted chicken back onto the table, but when he reached for it, it had turned into a large toad, which jumped into his face and sat there and never went away again. If anyone tried to remove it, it looked venomously at him as though it would jump into his face, so that no one dared to touch it. And the ungrateful son was forced to feed the toad every day, or else it would eat from his face. And thus, he went to and fro in the world without rest.

7. Part A
What is the theme of this story?

Ⓐ The theme of the story is to always share what you have to share.

Ⓑ The theme of the story is to not be afraid of toads because they can keep you from saving someone's life.

Ⓒ The theme of the story is that you should always feed yourself first, and then you will be strong enough to help others.

Ⓓ The theme of the story is that you should always share your chicken with your parents.

Part B
The theme of "The Ungrateful Son" is implied because _____.

Ⓐ It is indirectly stated, and the reader has to determine the theme through the actions of the characters.

Ⓑ It is explicitly stated and the reader does not have to guess at all.

Ⓒ It is obvious and doesn't require much thought.

Ⓓ None of the above

The Fox and the Crow Aesop's Fable

A Fox once saw a Crow fly off with a piece of cheese in its beak and settle on a branch of a tree. "That's for me, as I am a Fox," said Master Reynard, and he walked up to the foot of the tree. "Good-day, Mistress Crow," he cried. "How well you are looking today: how glossy your feathers; how bright your eye. I feel sure your voice must surpass that of other birds, just as your figure does; let me hear but one song from you that I may greet you as the Queen of Birds." The Crow lifted up her head and began to caw her best, but the moment she opened her mouth, the piece of cheese fell to the ground, only to be snapped up by Master Fox. "That will do," said he. "That was all I wanted. In exchange for your cheese, I will give you a piece of advice for the future."

8. What is the theme of this story?

Ⓐ Help out your friends.
Ⓑ Don't trust flatterers.
Ⓒ Sometimes, a song is necessary.
Ⓓ You should never have to work for food.

Question 9 is based on the story below

After reading the story, enter the details in the map below. This will help you to answer the questions that follow.

Walk-A-Thon

It was clear there weren't enough funds for the 8th-grade graduation ceremony at the end of the year. Big deal – why should I care? I was on the student council, but I never cared about graduation ceremonies.
It costs about $5,000.00 for the rent, equipment, the insurance, and all the other incidentals that pile up when planning a large event. Principal Dorsey told us that he didn't have the money this year. He said that if we wanted to keep the graduation tradition going, we would have to raise the money ourselves. "I'm sure we can live without the ceremony, but it would be nice to have," he told us. Then he left the meeting.

Immediately, Katrina Reynolds shot her hand in the air. She's not very popular, and I always feel kind of sorry for her. "We have to do this, you guys," Katrina gushed. "There is no way we are going to be the only class ever not to have a graduation ceremony."

Then, of course, Abbie Morelle, who was President, shot her hand in the air. I'd been on Student Council for two years, and as far as I could remember, Abbie had never let Katrina say anything without disagreeing with it. "It's very late in the year," Abbie said. "And we already have the Band Land Dance scheduled, which we don't have enough money for. We can't raise $7,000 in, like, two months."

Paulie Roman, who was treasurer, said, "According to my records, it would be more like $7,012, although we can't be certain of the precise cost of unspecified expenses related to the ceremony."

I didn't care. To me, 8th-grade is pure misery, no matter what you do. If you have a great graduation ceremony at the end of it, that's like saying, "We had such a great time in all of our boring classes and with all of the bullies every day. Let's have a party to celebrate them!" But I was all for a fundraiser if it would get Abbie Morelle off Katrina's back.

I said, "Let's do a walk-a-thon. We could raise a lot of money that way."

"Walk-a-thons are stupid," Abbie said.

Paulie Roman asked, "How much money could we raise with a walk-a-thon?"

I said, "When we did a walk-a-thon for cancer research in elementary school, we raised $4,000. This school is twice as big, and people can walk farther."

"Yeah," Abbie said, "but that was for cancer. Why would anyone give us money for a graduation ceremony? Plus, someone has to organize it, and it's complicated."

That got me mad enough that I had to say, "It's not that complicated. I'll do it."

What was I thinking? I spent the next month doing almost nothing except organizing that walk-a-thon. I hate walk-a-thons, and I hate talking to people about money. I ended up doing way more than I ever wanted to.

Within the first two weeks, I could see that we weren't going to get enough. It was because we weren't raising money for something important, like cancer. So I started telling people that the money would also go for cancer research. Then, when I saw how many people were ready to give more, I just told them it was all for cancer research. I got hundreds of parents signed up, and I got businesses to donate food and decorations.

Abbie was completely jealous.

The walk-a-thon was almost a success, too. But the day before, Principal Dorsey called me into his office. He wanted to know if it was true that I had been telling people that the money would go to cancer research because he had understood the money was going for our 8th-grade graduation party. I didn't answer. He said that he was going to call some of the people who pledged money to ask them if I had said anything about cancer.

"It was the only way I could raise enough money!" I answered back, knowing the lie had caught up with me.

"Well, it was the wrong thing to do." Principal Dorsey replied. "Now, you are going to have to contact every person who donated and let them know the truth. You also may not have enough money for a graduation party now."

I knew I should never have volunteered to lead this.

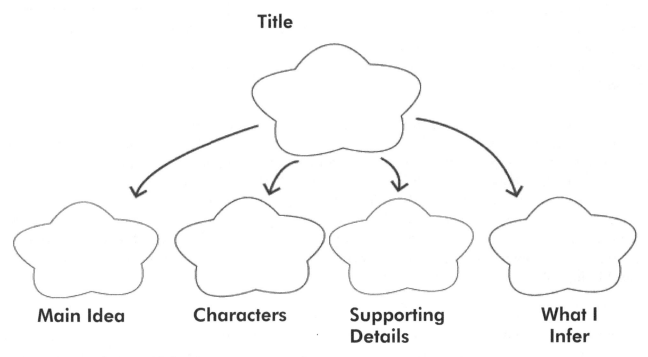

Title

Main Idea   Characters   Supporting Details   What I Infer

9. What is the theme of this story?

Ⓐ Don't volunteer to do things.
Ⓑ Principals can be very stern.
Ⓒ Make sure your intentions are pure, or the results will be disastrous.
Ⓓ Walk-a-thons are not the best money-makers.

Question 10 is based on the story below

The Laundry

Charlie's parents always assigned him chores around the house. They would often ask him to trim the lawn, wash the dishes, and feed the dog. However, his chores never included laundry. He relied on his mother to wash his clothes for him. Charlie was an outstanding student and was recently accepted to a top college. The college he planned to attend was in New York City. Charlie was nervous about leaving Texas, where he grew up, and being so far away from his family, but he knew that the college in New York was the perfect fit for him. Before he left, his mother decided that she had better show him how to wash his own clothes because she wouldn't be there to do it for him anymore. She showed Charlie how to sort his clothes into two piles: whites and colors.

Then she showed him how much soap to use and told him when to use hot or warm water and when to use cold water. Next, she explained the different settings on the dryer and told him to be careful not to dry certain items on high heat. Charlie didn't pay much attention. He didn't see what could happen or what was so complicated about washing clothes. He planned on packing mostly t-shirts and jeans and figured that it would be hard to mess up something so simple. When Charlie arrived at school, he was completely overwhelmed with all of the exciting things to do and new people to meet. He was also careful to dedicate plenty of time to his schoolwork because he wanted to impress his professors and earn good grades.

One morning Charlie woke up and found that he had no clean clothes to wear. His schedule had been so packed with activities and studying that he had managed to get through the first month of school without doing any laundry. That night, Charlie piled his soiled clothes into a large basket and headed to his dormitory's laundry room. He shoved all of his clothes into a washer, poured in the soap, and pressed the start. Half an hour later, he opened the washer and started moving the clothes into the dryer. It was then that he realized that he had skipped one very significant step. All of his white t-shirts and socks had turned pink. He had forgotten to sort his colors from his whites. Charlie had received a bright red t-shirt with his new school's logo across the front. The red dye had bled in the wash, turning all of his white clothes pink.

Charlie was unhappy about his destroyed wardrobe, but he figured that there was absolutely nothing to do except to put the clothes in the dryer and hope for the best. So he transferred the clothes to a dryer and set the heat to high. After all, he was anxious to get back upstairs to his studies. An hour later, Charlie removed his clothes from the dryer and headed straight back to his dorm room. The following morning, he reached for one of his favorite t-shirts. It was slightly pink now, but he didn't have enough money to replace all of his newly pink clothes. He would have to wear them, pink or not. As he pulled the shirt over his head, he noticed that it seemed tight. He looked at himself in the mirror.

The shirt had shrunk in the dryer. It looked like he had tried to squeeze into his little sister's pink t-shirt. All Charlie could do was laugh. He called his mom and asked her to repeat her laundry instructions again.

This time, Charlie took notes.

10. What is the theme of this story?

Ⓐ Pay close attention when you are learning something new.
Ⓑ Always ask for help.
Ⓒ Learn how to do your laundry when you are young.
Ⓓ Always have your parents do your laundry.

Test ID	8E004
Test Name	**Objective Summary**
Student Name	
Date	

1	Ⓐ Ⓑ Ⓒ Ⓓ	6	Ⓐ Ⓑ Ⓒ Ⓓ	11	Answer in the space provided below.
2	Ⓐ Ⓑ Ⓒ Ⓓ	7	Ⓐ Ⓑ Ⓒ Ⓓ	12	Answer in the space provided below.
3	Ⓐ Ⓑ Ⓒ Ⓓ	8	Ⓐ Ⓑ Ⓒ Ⓓ		
4	Ⓐ Ⓑ Ⓒ Ⓓ	9	Ⓐ Ⓑ Ⓒ Ⓓ		
5	Answer in the space provided below.	10	Ⓐ Ⓑ Ⓒ Ⓓ		

5

11

12

Chapter 1 → Lesson 4: Objective Summary

1. What is an objective summary?

- Ⓐ a restatement of the main idea of a text with the addition of the writer's opinion on the idea
- Ⓑ a restatement of the main idea of a text without the addition of the writer's opinion of the idea
- Ⓒ a paraphrase of the text with a focus on the writer's opinion and how it affects the main idea of the passage
- Ⓓ a paraphrase of the text with a focus on the reader's opinion

2. An objective summary should _____ .

- Ⓐ include supporting details
- Ⓑ be brief, accurate, and objective
- Ⓒ include both main points and supporting details
- Ⓓ include the reader's opinion of the text

3. An objective summary should always _____ .

- Ⓐ clearly show your opinions of the text
- Ⓑ clearly communicate a summary of the text
- Ⓒ clearly indicate all the characters in the text
- Ⓓ include at least four sentences

Question 4 is based on the passage below

It had been a year since Lauren had seen Bailey. Bailey's family had moved to Qatar leaving Lauren to face the world without her best friend. Anxiously, Lauren waited at the arrival gate hoping to glimpse a peek at her childhood friend. She knew after eleven hours in the air, Bailey would be exhausted; but, she could hardly wait to catch up. Moments later, the doors to the gate flung open, and there was her best friend, Bailey.

Once home, the hours passed like minutes as the girls laughed and giggled sharing moments from the last year. It felt as if they had never been apart. But Lauren felt like Bailey was holding something back.

4. What is the best summary for this passage?

- Ⓐ After a year abroad, Lauren was excited about seeing her best friend and catching up.
- Ⓑ Lauren was too excited about seeing her best friend Bailey, and even though she knew Bailey was tired from her flight, she probably talked her ear off.
- Ⓒ Bailey had been gone a year.
- Ⓓ Bailey was Lauren's best friend and though she had been gone a year, she really didn't want to come back.

After reading the story, enter the details in the map below. This will help you to answer the questions that follow.

The Ungrateful Son
by Jacob and Wilhelm Grimm

Once, a man was sitting with his wife before their front door. They had a roasted chicken which they were about to eat together. Then the man saw that his aged father was approaching, and he hastily took the chicken and hid it, for he did not want to share it with him. The old man came, had a drink, and went away. Now the son wanted to put the roasted chicken back onto the table, but when he reached for it, it had turned into a large toad, which jumped into his face and sat there and never went away again. If anyone tried to remove it, it looked venomously at him as though it would jump into his face, so that no one dared to touch it. And the ungrateful son was forced to feed the toad every day, or else it would eat from his face. And thus he went to and fro in the world without rest.

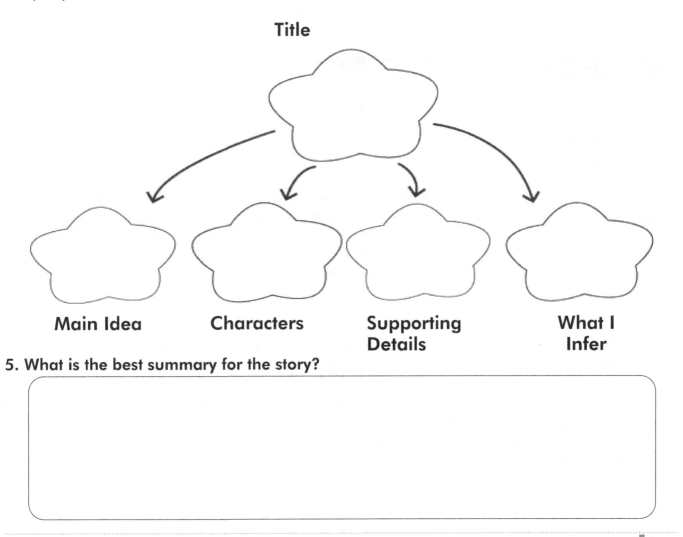

5. What is the best summary for the story?

Question 6 is based on the passage below

When I was finished with my doctor's appointment, I made my way to the lobby. My mom was going to pick me up, but knowing how she was always late, I realized I had some time to spare. I took a seat in the lobby and smiled politely at the three elderly people sitting near me. There were two women and an old man. Then I dug into my backpack for my library book.

Soon, one of the women and the man left. It was just me and the beautiful gray-haired woman in the lobby.

6. What is the best summary for this passage?

 Ⓐ A boy went to the lobby and waits for his mother.
 Ⓑ After a doctor's appointment, the narrator waits in the lobby for his mother to pick him up. At the end, only he and a woman remain in the lobby.
 Ⓒ The narrator, who must be impatient, waits for his mother in the lobby.
 Ⓓ The narrator reads a library book in the lobby while waiting for his mother.

Question 7 is based on the passage below

The Laundry

Charlie's parents always assigned him chores around the house. They would often ask him to trim the lawn, wash the dishes, and feed the dog. However, his chores never included laundry. He relied on his mother to wash his clothes for him. Charlie was an outstanding student and was recently accepted to a top college. The college he planned to attend was in New York City. Charlie was nervous about leaving Texas, where he grew up, and being so far away from his family, but he knew that the college in New York was the perfect fit for him. Before he left, his mother decided that she had better show him how to wash his own clothes because she wouldn't be there to do it for him anymore. She showed Charlie how to sort his clothes into two piles: whites and colors.

7. What is the best summary for this story?

 Ⓐ Charlie is going away to college and is nervous about not being in Texas anymore.
 Ⓑ Charlie is going to New York City for college. He has done many chores in the past but not laundry.
 Ⓒ Charlie is going to college in New York City and needs to learn how to do his laundry before he leaves. His mother teaches him how to sort his clothes.
 Ⓓ Charlie has done many chores in the past. He is nervous about leaving Texas but knows the college he is going to will be a good fit.

Question 8 is based on the passage below

From **Chapter 5 of Peter Pan** by J.M. Barrie

"He lay at his ease in a rough chariot drawn and propelled by his men, and instead of a right hand, he had the iron hook with which ever and anon he encouraged them to increase their pace. As dogs, this terrible man treated and addressed them, and as dogs, they obeyed him. In-person he was ca-daverous [dead looking] and [dark faced], and his hair was dressed in long curls, which at a little distance looked like black candles, and gave a singularly threatening expression to his handsome countenance. His eyes were of the blue of the forget-me-not, and of a profound melancholy, save when he was plunging his hook into you, at which time two red spots appeared in them and lit them up horribly. A man of indomitable courage, it was said that the only thing he shied at was the sight of his own blood, which was thick and of an unusual color. But undoubtedly the grimmest part of him was his iron claw."

8. Which choice best summarizes the personality of the character in the following excerpt?

Ⓐ James Hook was a scary man because he had the face of a dead person and had dark curly hair and a hook for his right hand. He treated his men like dogs, and they obeyed him as such. When he was angry, his eyes turned from blue to red.

Ⓑ James Hook used his appearance to assert his authority in ways that forced others into doing what he wanted. He spoke to and treated his men like dogs, and they were forced to listen. Only the sight of his own blood could waver his courage.

Ⓒ James Hook was a scary man.

Ⓓ James Hook was a scary man. James Hook used his appearance to assert his authority in ways that forced others into doing what he wanted. He spoke to and treated his men like dogs, and they were forced to listen. Only the sight of his own blood could waver his courage.

Question 9 is based on the passage below

The Emperor Penguin is the only penguin species that breeds during the Antarctic winter. It treks 31–75 miles over the ice to breeding colonies, which may include thousands of penguins. The female lays a single egg, which is then incubated by the male while the female returns to the sea to feed; parents subsequently take turns foraging at sea and caring for their chick in the colony. The average lifespan of the Emperor Penguin is 20 years, although observations suggest that some Emperor Penguins may live to 50 years of age.

9. **Read the summary below. Select the answer below that best explains why the summary provided cannot be considered a proper objective summary.**

> Breeding during the winter in Antarctica is specific to the Emperor Penguin. The Emperor Penguin travels far; they will travel anywhere from 31 – 75 miles in the freezing cold to meet many other penguins for breeding. This is known as a breeding colony and a colony can have thousands of penguins. The father penguins sit on the eggs while the mothers go and hunt for food at sea. After the chick is born, the mother and father take turns taking care of the baby and going off to feed. Emperor Penguins, on average, live to be about 20 years old, but some have been known to live up to 50 years.

Ⓐ The summary is incorrect because it includes the writer's opinion.
Ⓑ The summary is perfect and should be considered proper.
Ⓒ The summary is incorrect because it is not a summary; it is a paraphrase of the passage.
Ⓓ The summary is incorrect because it is not accurate.

Question 10 is based on the story below

After reading the story, enter the details in the map below. This will help you to answer the questions that follow.

Walk-A-Thon

It was clear there weren't enough funds for the 8th-grade graduation ceremony at the end of the year. Big deal – why should I care? I was on the Student Council, but I never cared about graduation ceremonies.

It costs about $5,000.00 for the rent, equipment, the insurance, and all the other incidentals that pile up when planning a large event. Principal Dorsey told us that he didn't have the money this year. He said that if we wanted to keep the graduation tradition going, we would have to raise the money ourselves. "I'm sure we can live without the ceremony, but it would be nice to have," he told us. Then he left the meeting.

Immediately, Katrina Reynolds shot her hand in the air. She's not very popular and I always feel kind of sorry for her. "We have to do this, you guys," Katrina gushed. "There is no way we are going to be the only class ever not to have a graduation ceremony."

Then, of course, Abbie Morelle, who was President, shot her hand in the air. I'd been on Student Council for two years and as far as I could remember, Abbie had never let Katrina say anything without disagreeing with it. "It's very late in the year," Abbie said. "And we already have the Band Land Dance scheduled, which we don't have enough money for. We can't raise $7,000 in, like, two months."

Paulie Roman, who was treasurer, said, "According to my records, it would be more like $7,012, although we can't be certain of the precise cost of unspecified expenses related to the ceremony."

I didn't care. To me, 8th-grade is pure misery, no matter what you do. If you have a great graduation ceremony at the end of it, that's like saying, "We had such a great time in all of our boring classes, and with all of the bullies every day. Let's have a party to celebrate them!" But I was all for a fundraiser if it would get Abbie Morelle off Katrina's back.

I said, "Let's do a walk-a-thon. We could raise a lot of money that way."

"Walk-a-thons are stupid," Abbie said.

Paulie Roman asked, "How much money could we raise with a walk-a-thon?"

I said, "When we did a walk-a-thon for cancer research in elementary school, we raised $4,000. This school is twice as big and people can walk farther."

"Yeah," Abbie said, "but that was for cancer. Why would anyone give us money for a graduation ceremony? Plus, someone has to organize it, and it's complicated."

That got me mad enough that I had to say, "It's not that complicated. I'll do it."

What was I thinking? I spent the next month doing almost nothing except organizing that walk-a-thon. I hate walk-a-thons, and I hate talking to people about money. I ended up doing way more than I ever wanted to.

Within the first two weeks I could see that we weren't going to get enough. It was because we weren't raising money for something important, like cancer. So I started telling people that the money would also go for cancer research. Then, when I saw how many people were ready to give more, I just told them it was all for cancer research. I got hundreds of parents signed up, and I got businesses to donate food and decorations.

Abbie was completely jealous.

The walk-a-thon was almost a success, too. But the day before, Principal Dorsey called me into his office. He wanted to know if it was true that I had been telling people that the money would go to cancer research, because he had understood the money was going to our 8th-grade graduation party. I didn't answer. He said that he was going to call some of the people who pledged money to ask them if I had said anything about cancer.

"It was the only way I could raise enough money!" I answered back, knowing the lie had caught up with me.

"Well, it was the wrong thing to do." Principal Dorsey replied. "Now, you are going to have to contact every person who donated and let them know the truth. You also may not have enough money for a graduation party now."

I knew I should never have volunteered to lead this.

Title

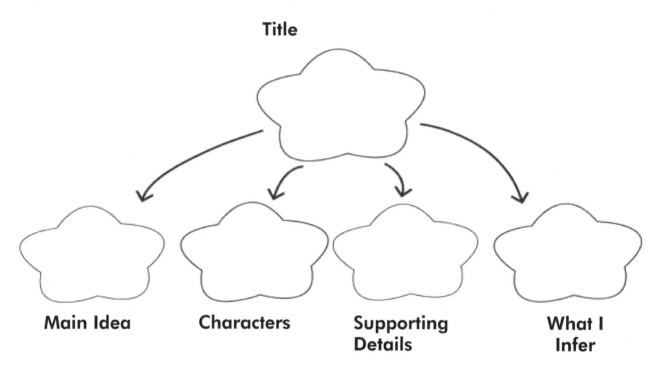

Main Idea   **Characters**   **Supporting Details**   **What I Infer**

10. Which is the best summary of the story?

Ⓐ   Student Council members learn that they do not have enough money for an 8th-grade graduation ceremony. They decide to raise money through a walk-a-thon which the narrator volunteers to lead.

Ⓑ   Student Council members learn that they do not have enough money for an 8th-grade graduation ceremony. They decide to raise money through a walk-a-thon which the narrator volunteers to lead. Fund raising doesn't go as well as anticipated and the 8th-grade graduation party is in jeopardy. The Student Council members were probably really mad after all their hard work.

Ⓒ   The 8th-grade class did not have enough money for a graduation party. They tried to raise money, but failed.

Ⓓ   Student Council members learn that they do not have enough money for an 8th-grade graduation ceremony. They decide to raise money through a walk-a-thon which the narrator volunteers to lead. Fund raising doesn't go as well as anticipated and the 8th-grade graduation party is in jeopardy.

The Ant and the Grasshopper Aesop's Fable

In a field, one summer's day, a grasshopper was hopping about, chirping and singing to its heart's content. A group of ants walked by, grunting as they struggled to carry plump kernels of corn. "Where are you going with those heavy things?" asked the grasshopper. Without stopping, the first ant replied, "To our anthill. This is the third kernel I've delivered today."

"Why not come and sing with me," teased the grasshopper, "instead of working so hard?"

"We are helping to store food for the winter," said the ant, "and think you should do the same."

"Winter is far away, and it is a glorious day to play," sang the grasshopper. But the ants went on their way and continued their hard work.

The weather soon turned cold. All the food lying in the field was covered with a thick white blanket of snow that even the grasshopper could not dig through.

Soon the grasshopper found itself dying of hunger. He staggered to the ants' hill and saw them handing out corn from the stores they had collected in the summer. He begged them for something to eat.

"What!" cried the ants in surprise, "haven't you stored anything away for the winter? What in the world were you doing all last summer?"

"I didn't have time to store any food," complained the grasshopper; "I was so busy playing music that before I knew, it the summer was gone."

The ants shook their heads in disgust, turned their backs on the grasshopper, and went on with their work.

11. What is the best summary for the story?

When I was finished with my doctor's appointment, I made my way to the lobby. My mom was going to pick me up, but knowing how she was always late, I realized I had some time to spare. I took a seat in the lobby and smiled politely at the three elderly people sitting near me. There were two women and an old man. Then I dug into my backpack for my library book.

Soon, one of the women and the man left. It was just me and the beautiful gray- haired woman in the lobby.

12. What is the best summary for the story?

Test ID	8E005
Test Name	Plot
Student Name	
Date	

1	Ⓐ Ⓑ Ⓒ Ⓓ	5 A	Ⓐ Ⓑ Ⓒ Ⓓ
2	Ⓐ Ⓑ Ⓒ Ⓓ	5 B	Ⓐ Ⓑ Ⓒ Ⓓ
3	Ⓐ Ⓑ Ⓒ Ⓓ	6 A	Ⓐ Ⓑ Ⓒ Ⓓ
4 A	Ⓐ Ⓑ Ⓒ Ⓓ	6 B	Ⓐ Ⓑ Ⓒ Ⓓ
4 B	Ⓐ Ⓑ Ⓒ Ⓓ	7	Ⓐ Ⓑ Ⓒ Ⓓ

Chapter 1 → Lesson 5: Plot

1. What are the elements of plot?

- Ⓐ prelude, beginning, interlude, middle, end
- Ⓑ exposition, setting, action, conflict, falling action
- Ⓒ exposition, rising action, climax, falling action, resolution
- Ⓓ beginning, middle, end

2. What are the two main types of conflict?

- Ⓐ internal and external
- Ⓑ interior and exterior
- Ⓒ good and bad
- Ⓓ big and little

3. What is the plot of a story?

- Ⓐ the message that the author is trying to convey
- Ⓑ the series of events that make up the story
- Ⓒ the use of characters in a story
- Ⓓ the part of a story where the characters decide what they are going to do

Question 4-7 are based on the story below

Walk-A-Thon

It was clear there weren't enough funds for the 8th-grade graduation ceremony at the end of the year. Big deal – why should I care? I was on the student council, but I never cared about graduation ceremonies.

It costs about $5,000.00 for the rent, equipment, the insurance, and all the other incidentals that pile up when planning a large event. Principal Dorsey told us that he didn't have the money this year. He said that if we wanted to keep the graduation tradition going, we would have to raise the money ourselves. "I'm sure we can live without the ceremony, but it would be nice to have," he told us. Then he left the meeting.

Immediately, Katrina Reynolds shot her hand in the air. She's not very popular, and I always feel kind of sorry for her. "We have to do this, you guys," Katrina gushed. "There is no way we are going to be the only class ever not to have a graduation ceremony."

Then, of course, Abbie Morelle, who was President, shot her hand in the air. I'd been on Student Council for two years, and as far as I could remember, Abbie had never let Katrina say anything without disagreeing with it. "It's very late in the year," Abbie said. "And we already have the Band Land Dance scheduled, which we don't have enough money for. We can't raise $7,000 in, like, two months."

Paulie Roman, who was treasurer, said, "According to my records, it would be more like $7,012, although we can't be certain of the precise cost of unspecified expenses related to the ceremony."

I didn't care. To me, 8th-grade is pure misery, no matter what you do. If you have a great graduation ceremony at the end of it, that's like saying, "We had such a great time in all of our boring classes and with all of the bullies every day. Let's have a party to celebrate them!" But I was all for a fundraiser if it would get Abbie Morelle off Katrina's back.

I said, "Let's do a walk-a-thon. We could raise a lot of money that way."

"Walk-a-thons are stupid," Abbie said.

Paulie Roman asked, "How much money could we raise with a walk-a-thon?"

I said, "When we did a walk-a-thon for cancer research in elementary school, we raised $4,000. This school is twice as big, and people can walk farther."

"Yeah," Abbie said, "but that was for cancer. Why would anyone give us money for a graduation ceremony? Plus, someone has to organize it, and it's complicated."

That got me mad enough that I had to say, "It's not that complicated. I'll do it."

What was I thinking? I spent the next month doing almost nothing except organizing that walk-a-thon. I hate walk-a-thons, and I hate talking to people about money. I ended up doing way more than I ever wanted to.

Within the first two weeks, I could see that we weren't going to get enough. It was because we weren't raising money for something important, like cancer. So I started telling people that the money would also go for cancer research. Then, when I saw how many people were ready to give more, I just told them it was all for cancer research. I got hundreds of parents signed up, and I got businesses to donate food and decorations.

Abbie was completely jealous.

The walk-a-thon was almost a success, too. But the day before, Principal Dorsey called me into his office. He wanted to know if it was true that I had been telling people that the money would go to cancer research because he had understood the money was going for our 8th-grade graduation party. I didn't answer. He said that he was going to call some of the people who pledged money to ask them if I had said anything about cancer.

"It was the only way I could raise enough money!" I answered back, knowing the lie had caught up with me.

"Well, it was the wrong thing to do." Principal Dorsey replied. "Now, you are going to have to contact every person who donated and let them know the truth. You also may not have enough money for a graduation party now."

I knew I should never have volunteered to lead this.

4. Part A
What is the major type of conflict in this story?

- Ⓐ external: man vs fate
- Ⓑ external: man vs man
- Ⓒ internal: man vs himself
- Ⓓ external: man vs nature

Part B
What is the conflict in this story?

- Ⓐ there is not enough money for an 8th-grade graduation party
- Ⓑ who is most popular
- Ⓒ who will organize the walk-a-thon
- Ⓓ whether or not to have graduation

5. Part A
What is the exposition in this story?

- Ⓐ I didn't care. To me, 8th-grade is pure misery, no matter what you do. If you have a great graduation ceremony at the end of it, that's like saying, "We had such a great time in all of our boring classes, and with all of the bullies every day. Let's have a party to celebrate them!" But I was all for a fundraiser if it would get Abbie Morelle off Katrina's back.

- Ⓑ He wanted to know if it was true that I had been telling people that the money would go to cancer research, because he had understood the money was going for our 8th-grade graduation party.

- Ⓒ Principal Dorsey told us that he didn't have the money this year. He said that if we wanted to keep the graduation tradition going, we would have to raise the money ourselves.

- Ⓓ It was clear there weren't enough funds for the 8th-grade graduation ceremony at the end of the year. Big deal – why should I care? I was on the Student Council, but I never cared about graduation ceremonies.

Part B
What is the most important event in the rising action of this story?

Ⓐ when the narrator volunteers to take charge of the walk-a-thon
Ⓑ when the narrator lies about why she is collecting the money
Ⓒ when the narrator gets called into the principal's office
Ⓓ when the principal says there will be no graduation

6. **Part A**
What is the climax of this story?

Ⓐ when the narrator volunteers to be in charge of the walk-a-thon
Ⓑ when the narrator lies about why she is collecting the money
Ⓒ when the principal calls the narrator to the office and the narrator confesses to lying about the cause
Ⓓ when the narrator makes Abbie jealous

Part B
What is the most important event in the falling action of this story?

Ⓐ when the narrator learns she must contact all the donors
Ⓑ when the narrator learns there will be no graduation party
Ⓒ when the narrator makes Abbie jealous
Ⓓ when the narrator organizes the walk-a-thon

7. **What is the resolution of this story?**

Ⓐ when the narrator volunteers to be in charge of the walk-a-thon
Ⓑ when the narrator is called to the principal's office
Ⓒ when the narrator learns there will be no graduation party
Ⓓ when Abbie gets jealous

Test ID	8E006
Test Name	**Setting**
Student Name	
Date	

1	Ⓐ Ⓑ Ⓒ Ⓓ	6	Ⓐ Ⓑ Ⓒ Ⓓ	11	Answer in the space provided below.
2	Ⓐ Ⓑ Ⓒ Ⓓ	7	Answer in the space provided below.		
3	Ⓐ Ⓑ Ⓒ Ⓓ	8	Ⓐ Ⓑ Ⓒ Ⓓ		
4	Ⓐ Ⓑ Ⓒ Ⓓ	9	Ⓐ Ⓑ Ⓒ Ⓓ		
5	Ⓐ Ⓑ Ⓒ Ⓓ	10	Ⓐ Ⓑ Ⓒ Ⓓ		

7

11

Chapter 1 → Lesson 6: Setting

1. During which part of a story is the setting usually introduced?

Ⓐ exposition
Ⓑ rising action
Ⓒ climax
Ⓓ resolution

2. Can there be more than one setting in a story?

Ⓐ yes
Ⓑ no
Ⓒ only if the story is really long
Ⓓ only if the story is really short

3. Which of the following can convey setting?

Ⓐ the name of the characters
Ⓑ the age of the characters
Ⓒ the culture of the characters
Ⓓ the thoughts of a character

4. What does the setting tell us about a story?

Ⓐ the names of the characters
Ⓑ the time and place of action in the story
Ⓒ the mood of the story
Ⓓ None of the above

Question 5 is based on the story below

Megan couldn't believe her luck. She had been standing in line with her best friend Jessica for thirty minutes. Their excitement was mounting as they neared the front of the line for the famed Greased Lightning roller coaster. Just as they took their seats, the clouds opened up. Soaking wet and disappointed, the girls followed the directions of the ride employees and took shelter under the nearby canopies.

5. Which of the following does not help the reader to gain a sense of the setting?

Ⓐ the time of day
Ⓑ the weather
Ⓒ the time of year
Ⓓ the mood of the main character

Question 6 is based on the passage below.

It had been a year since Lauren had seen Bailey. Bailey's family had moved to Qatar leaving Lauren to face the world without her best friend. Anxiously, Lauren waited at the arrival gate hoping to glimpse a peek at her childhood friend. She knew after eleven hours in the air, Bailey would be exhausted; but, she could hardly wait to catch up. Moments later, the doors to the gate flung open, and there was her best friend, Bailey.

Once home, the hours passed like minutes as the girls laughed and giggled sharing moments from the last year. It felt as if they had never been apart. But Lauren felt like Bailey was holding something back.

6. What is the primary setting for this passage?

Ⓐ an airport
Ⓑ Lauren's house
Ⓒ Bailey's house
Ⓓ There is not enough information to determine the setting.

Question 7 is based on the paragraph below

From **Chapter 5 of Peter Pan** by J.M. Barrie

"He lay at his ease in a rough chariot drawn and propelled by his men, and instead of a right hand, he had the iron hook with which ever and anon he encouraged them to increase their pace. As dogs, this terrible man treated and addressed them, and as dogs, they obeyed him. In-person he was cadaverous [dead looking] and [dark faced], and his hair was dressed in long curls, which at a little distance looked like black candles, and gave a singularly threatening expression to his handsome countenance. His eyes were of the blue of the forget-me-not, and of a profound melancholy, save when he was plunging his hook into you, at which time two red spots appeared in them and lit them up horribly. A man of indomitable courage, it was said that the only thing he shied at was the sight of his own blood, which was thick and of an unusual color. But undoubtedly the grimmest part of him was his iron claw."

7. What is the setting of the above paragraph from the excerpt?

The Laundry

Charlie's parents always assigned him chores around the house. They would often ask him to trim the lawn, wash the dishes, and feed the dog. However, his chores never included laundry. He relied on his mother to wash his clothes for him. Charlie was an outstanding student and was recently accepted to a top college. The college he planned to attend was in New York City. Charlie was nervous about leaving Texas, where he grew up, and being so far away from his family; but, he knew that the college in New York was the perfect fit for him. Before he left, his mother decided that she had better show him how to wash his own clothes because she wouldn't be there to do it for him anymore. She showed Charlie how to sort his clothes into two piles: whites and colors.

Then she showed him how much soap to use and told him when to use hot or warm water and when to use cold water. Next, she explained the different settings on the dryer and told him to be careful not to dry certain items on high heat. Charlie didn't pay much attention. He didn't see what could happen or what was so complicated about washing clothes. He planned on packing mostly t-shirts and jeans and figured that it would be hard to mess up something so simple.

When Charlie arrived at school, he was completely overwhelmed with all of the exciting things to do and new people to meet. He was also careful to dedicate plenty of time to his schoolwork because he wanted to impress his professors and earn good grades.

One morning Charlie woke up and found that he had no clean clothes to wear. His schedule had been so packed with activities and studying that he had managed to get through the first month of school without doing any laundry. That night, Charlie piled his soiled clothes into a large basket and headed to his dormitory's laundry room. He shoved all of his clothes into a washer, poured in the soap, and pressed the start. Half an hour later, he opened the washer and started moving the clothes into the dryer. It was then that he realized that he had skipped one very significant step. All of his white t-shirts and socks had turned pink. He had forgotten to sort his colors from his whites. Charlie had received a bright red t-shirt with his new school's logo across the front. The red dye had bled in the wash, turning all of his white clothes pink.

Charlie was unhappy about his destroyed wardrobe, but he figured that there was absolutely nothing to do except to put the clothes in the dryer and hope for the best. So he transferred the clothes to a dryer and set the heat to high. After all, he was anxious to get back upstairs to his studies. An hour later, Charlie removed his clothes from the dryer and headed straight back to his dorm room. The following morning, he reached for one of his favorite t-shirts. It was slightly pink now, but he didn't have enough money to replace all of his newly pink clothes. He would have to wear them, pink or not. As he pulled the shirt over his head, he noticed that it seemed tight. He looked at himself in the mirror. The shirt had shrunk in the dryer. It looked like he had tried to squeeze into his little sister's pink t-shirt. All Charlie could do was laugh. He called his mom and asked her to repeat her laundry instructions again.

This time, Charlie took notes.

8. What is the first setting of this excerpt?

Ⓐ Texas
Ⓑ New York
Ⓒ a laundromat
Ⓓ There is not enough information to determine the setting.

Question 9 is based on the story below

I sat with my mother, a friendly and courageous woman, on the back porch of our country home. The thermometer read 100 degrees, and even the plants seemed to sweat in the heat.

9. Which of the following does not help the reader to better understand the setting of the story?

Ⓐ "the back porch"
Ⓑ "thermometer read 100 degrees"
Ⓒ "a friendly and courageous woman"
Ⓓ "our country home"

Question 10 is based on the paragraph below

University of California Berkeley scientists confirmed that a cluster of fossilized bones found in Silicon Valley are likely the remains of a mammoth. The giant beast would have roamed the area between 10,000 and 40,000 years ago. A pair of elephant-like tusks, a huge pelvic bone, and the animal's rib cage were found by an amateur naturalist who was walking a dog along a canal near San Jose's Guadalupe River. It could be the remains of a Columbian mammoth, according to paleontologists who expect to study the site.

10. What is the setting of this article?

Ⓐ Columbia
Ⓑ University of California Berkeley
Ⓒ a canal near the Guadalupe River in the Silicon Valley
Ⓓ Berkeley

From Chapter 1 of Bullets and Billets by Bruce Bainsfather

Gliding up the Seine, on a transport crammed to the lid with troops, in the still, cold hours of a November morning, was my debut into the war. It was about 6 a.m. when our boat silently slipped along past the great wooden sheds, posts and complications of Havre Harbour. I had spent most of the twelve-hour trip down somewhere in the depths of the ship, dealing out rations to the hundred men that I had brought with me from Plymouth. This sounds a comparatively simple process, but not a bit of it. To begin with, the ship was filled with troops to bursting point, and the mere matter of proceeding from one deck to another was about as difficult as trying to get round to see a friend at the other side of the ground at a Crystal Palace Cup final.

11. What is the setting of this excerpt?

Test ID	8E007
Test Name	Character
Student Name	
Date	

1	Ⓐ Ⓑ Ⓒ Ⓓ	6 A	Ⓐ Ⓑ Ⓒ Ⓓ	9	Ⓐ Ⓑ Ⓒ Ⓓ		
2	Ⓐ Ⓑ Ⓒ Ⓓ	6 B	Ⓐ Ⓑ Ⓒ Ⓓ	10	Ⓐ Ⓑ Ⓒ Ⓓ		
3	Ⓐ Ⓑ Ⓒ Ⓓ	7 A	Ⓐ Ⓑ Ⓒ Ⓓ	11	Ⓐ Ⓑ Ⓒ Ⓓ		
4	Ⓐ Ⓑ Ⓒ Ⓓ	7 B	Ⓐ Ⓑ Ⓒ Ⓓ				
5	Ⓐ Ⓑ Ⓒ Ⓓ	8	Ⓐ Ⓑ Ⓒ Ⓓ				

Chapter 1 → Lesson 7: Character

1. What is a round character?

   Ⓐ a character who has many personality traits
   Ⓑ a character who has very few personality traits
   Ⓒ a character who changes throughout the story
   Ⓓ a character who does not change throughout the story

2. Who or what is the protagonist of a story?

   Ⓐ the main character with the problem
   Ⓑ the character that is the least interesting
   Ⓒ the character that is the most interesting
   Ⓓ main character's opposing force

3. Who or what is the antagonist in a story?

   Ⓐ the main character of a story
   Ⓑ the main character's opposing force
   Ⓒ the character that is the least interesting
   Ⓓ the character that is the most interesting

4. What is a static character?

   Ⓐ a character that changes during the course of the story
   Ⓑ a character that does not change during the course of the story
   Ⓒ a character with a smaller role that is not important to the development of the story
   Ⓓ a character with a large role that is not vital to the development of the story

5. What is a dynamic character?

   Ⓐ a character that changes during the course of the story
   Ⓑ a character that does not change during the course of the story
   Ⓒ a character with a smaller role that is not important to the development of the story
   Ⓓ a character with a large role that is not vital to the development of the story

Question 6 and 7 are based on the story below

Walk-A-Thon

It was clear there weren't enough funds for the 8th-grade graduation ceremony at the end of the year. Big deal – why should I care? I was on the student council, but I never cared about graduation ceremonies.

It costs about $5,000.00 for the rent, equipment, the insurance, and all the other incidentals that pile up when planning a large event. Principal Dorsey told us that he didn't have the money this year. He said that if we wanted to keep the graduation tradition going, we would have to raise the money ourselves. "I'm sure we can live without the ceremony, but it would be nice to have," he told us. Then he left the meeting.

Immediately, Katrina Reynolds shot her hand in the air. She's not very popular, and I always feel kind of sorry for her. "We have to do this, you guys," Katrina gushed. "There is no way we are going to be the only class ever not to have a graduation ceremony."

Then, of course, Abbie Morelle, who was President, shot her hand in the air. I'd been on Student Council for two years, and as far as I could remember, Abbie had never let Katrina say anything without disagreeing with it. "It's very late in the year," Abbie said. "And we already have the Band Land Dance scheduled, which we don't have enough money for. We can't raise $7,000 in, like, two months."

Paulie Roman, who was treasurer, said, "According to my records, it would be more like $7,012, although we can't be certain of the precise cost of unspecified expenses related to the ceremony."

I didn't care. To me, 8th-grade is pure misery, no matter what you do. If you have a great graduation ceremony at the end of it, that's like saying, "We had such a great time in all of our boring classes and with all of the bullies every day. Let's have a party to celebrate them!" But I was all for a fundraiser if it would get Abbie Morelle off Katrina's back.

I said, "Let's do a walk-a-thon. We could raise a lot of money that way."

"Walk-a-thons are stupid," Abbie said.
Paulie Roman asked, "How much money could we raise with a walk-a-thon?"

I said, "When we did a walk-a-thon for cancer research in elementary school, we raised $4,000. This school is twice as big, and people can walk farther."

"Yeah," Abbie said, "but that was for cancer. Why would anyone give us money for a graduation ceremony? Plus, someone has to organize it, and it's complicated."

That got me mad enough that I had to say, "It's not that complicated. I'll do it."

What was I thinking? I spent the next month doing almost nothing except organizing that walk-a-thon. I hate walk-a-thons, and I hate talking to people about money. I ended up doing way more than I ever wanted to.

Within the first two weeks, I could see that we weren't going to get enough. It was because we weren't raising money for something important, like cancer. So I started telling people that the money would also go for cancer research. Then, when I saw how many people were ready to give more, I just told them it was all for cancer research. I got hundreds of parents signed up, and I got businesses to donate food and decorations.

Abbie was completely jealous.

The walk-a-thon was almost a success, too. But the day before, Principal Dorsey called me into his office. He wanted to know if it was true that I had been telling people that the money would go to cancer research because he had understood the money was going for our 8th-grade graduation party. I didn't answer. He said that he was going to call some of the people who pledged money to ask them if I had said anything about cancer.

"It was the only way I could raise enough money!" I answered back, knowing the lie had caught up with me.

"Well, it was the wrong thing to do." Principal Dorsey replied. "Now, you are going to have to contact every person who donated and let them know the truth. You also may not have enough money for a graduation party now."

I knew I should never have volunteered to lead this.

6. Part A
What sort of character is the narrator?

Ⓐ major
Ⓑ minor
Ⓒ middle
Ⓓ weak

Part B
Who or what is the main antagonist in this story?

Ⓐ unnamed narrator
Ⓑ Abbie Morelle
Ⓒ Paulie Roman
Ⓓ none of the above

7. Part A
What sort of character is Principal Dorsey?

Ⓐ major
Ⓑ minor
Ⓒ middle
Ⓓ weak

Part B
What type of character is Abbie Morelle?

Ⓐ round
Ⓑ flat
Ⓒ bumpy
Ⓓ none of the above

Question 8 and 9 are based on the story below

Excerpt from **Stave One of A Christmas Carol** by Charles Dickens

(1) "What else can I be," returned the uncle [Scrooge], "when I live in such a world of fools as this? Merry Christmas! Out upon Merry Christmas! What's Christmas time to you but a time for paying bills without money; a time for finding yourself a year older, but not an hour richer; a time for balancing your books and having every item in 'em through a round dozen of months presented dead against you? If I could work my will," said Scrooge indignantly, "every idiot who goes about with 'Merry Christmas' on his lips should be boiled with his own pudding, and buried with a stake of holly through his heart. He should!"

Excerpt from **Stave Five of A Christmas Carol** by Charles Dickens

(2) "A merry Christmas, Bob!" said Scrooge [the uncle], with an earnestness that could not be mistaken, as he clapped him on the back. "A merrier Christmas, Bob, my good fellow, than I have given you, for many a year! I'll raise your salary, and endeavor to assist your struggling family, and we will discuss your affairs this very afternoon, over a Christmas bowl of smoking bishop, Bob! Make up the fires, and buy another coal-scuttle before you dot another, Bob Cratchit!"

8. What type of characterization does Dickens use to describe Scrooge (the uncle)?

Ⓐ indirect characterization
Ⓑ direct characterization
Ⓒ false characterization
Ⓓ none of the above

9. What type of character is Scrooge (the uncle)?

Ⓐ flat
Ⓑ static
Ⓒ round
Ⓓ dynamic

Question 10 and 11 are based on the story below

Excerpt from the **Foreword of A Princess of Mars** by Edgar Rice Burroughs

My first recollection of Captain Carter is of the few months he spent at my father's home in Virginia, just prior to the opening of the Civil War. I was then a child of but five years, yet I well remember the tall, dark, smooth-faced, athletic man whom I called Uncle Jack.

He seemed always to be laughing; and he entered into the sports of the children with the same hearty good fellowship he displayed toward those pastimes in which the men and women of his own age indulged; or he would sit for an hour at a time entertaining my old grandmother with stories of his strange, wild life in all parts of the world. We all loved him, and our slaves fairly worshipped the ground he trod.

He was a splendid specimen of manhood, standing a good two inches over six feet, broad of shoulder and narrow of hip, with the carriage of the trained fighting man. His features were regular and clear cut, his hair black and closely cropped, while his eyes were of a steel gray, reflecting a strong and loyal character, filled with fire and initiative. His manners were perfect, and his courtliness was that of a typical southern gentleman of the highest type.

His horsemanship, especially after hounds, was a marvel and delight even in that country of magnificent horsemen. I have often heard my father caution him against his wild recklessness, but he would only laugh, and say that the tumble that killed him would be from the back of a horse yet unfoaled. When the war broke out he left us, nor did I see him again for some fifteen or sixteen years. When he returned it was without warning, and I was much surprised to note that he had not aged apparently a moment, nor had he changed in any other outward way. He was, when others were with him, the same genial, happy fellow we had known of old, but when he thought himself alone I have seen him sit for hours gazing off into space, his face set in a look of wistful longing and hopeless misery; and at night he would sit thus looking up into the heavens, at what I did not know until I read his manuscript years afterward.

10. What sort of characterization is used in this excerpt?

Ⓐ direct characterization
Ⓑ indirect characterization
Ⓒ false characterization
Ⓓ none of the above

11. What type of character is Captain Carter?

Ⓐ flat
Ⓑ static
Ⓒ round
Ⓓ dynamic

Test ID	8E008
Test Name	**Analyzing Literature**
Student Name	
Date	

1	Ⓐ Ⓑ Ⓒ Ⓓ	**5**	Ⓐ Ⓑ Ⓒ Ⓓ	**8 C**	Ⓐ Ⓑ Ⓒ Ⓓ		
2 A	Ⓐ Ⓑ Ⓒ Ⓓ	**6**	Ⓐ Ⓑ Ⓒ Ⓓ				
2 B	Ⓐ Ⓑ Ⓒ Ⓓ	**7**	Ⓐ Ⓑ Ⓒ Ⓓ				
3	Ⓐ Ⓑ Ⓒ Ⓓ	**8 A**	Ⓐ Ⓑ Ⓒ Ⓓ				
4	Ⓐ Ⓑ Ⓒ Ⓓ	**8 B**	Ⓐ Ⓑ Ⓒ Ⓓ				

Chapter 1 → Lesson 8: Analyzing Literature

Question 1 and 2 are based on the story below

The Laundry

Charlie's parents always assigned him chores around the house. They would often ask him to trim the lawn, wash the dishes, and feed the dog. However, his chores never included laundry. He relied on his mother to wash his clothes for him. Charlie was an outstanding student and was recently accepted to a top college. The college he planned to attend was in New York City. Charlie was nervous about leaving Texas, where he grew up, and being so far away from his family; but, he knew that the college in New York was the perfect fit for him. Before he left, his mother decided that she had better show him how to wash his own clothes because she wouldn't be there to do it for him anymore. She showed Charlie how to sort his clothes into two piles: whites and colors.

Then she showed him how much soap to use and told him when to use hot or warm water and when to use cold water. Next, she explained the different settings on the dryer and told him to be careful not to dry certain items on high heat. Charlie didn't pay much attention. He didn't see what could happen or what was so complicated about washing clothes. He planned on packing mostly t-shirts and jeans and figured that it would be hard to mess up something so simple.

When Charlie arrived at school, he was completely overwhelmed with all of the exciting things to do and new people to meet. He was also careful to dedicate plenty of time to his schoolwork because he wanted to impress his professors and earn good grades.

One morning Charlie woke up and found that he had no clean clothes to wear. His schedule had been so packed with activities and studying that he had managed to get through the first month of school without doing any laundry. That night, Charlie piled his soiled clothes into a large basket and headed to his dormitory's laundry room. He shoved all of his clothes into a washer, poured in the soap, and pressed the start. Half an hour later, he opened the washer and started moving the clothes into the dryer. It was then that he realized that he had skipped one very significant step. All of his white t-shirts and socks had turned pink. He had forgotten to sort his colors from his whites. Charlie had received a bright red t-shirt with his new school's logo across the front. The red dye had bled in the wash, turning all of his white clothes pink.

Charlie was unhappy about his destroyed wardrobe, but he figured that there was absolutely nothing to do except to put the clothes in the dryer and hope for the best. So he transferred the clothes to a dryer and set the heat to high. After all, he was anxious to get back upstairs to his studies. An hour later, Charlie removed his clothes from the dryer and headed straight back to his dorm room. The following morning, he reached for one of his favorite t-shirts. It was slightly pink now, but he didn't have enough money to replace all of his newly pink clothes. He would have to wear them, pink or not. As he pulled the shirt over his head, he noticed that it seemed tight. He looked at himself in the mirror.

The shirt had shrunk in the dryer. It looked like he had tried to squeeze into his little sister's pink t-shirt. All Charlie could do was laugh. He called his mom and asked her to repeat her laundry instructions again.

This time, Charlie took notes.

1. Which statement best describes Charlie's parents' expectations of him?

Ⓐ They let Charlie do whatever he wants since he's smart and will probably make good decisions.
Ⓑ They expect Charlie to help around the house and earn good grades in school.
Ⓒ They don't expect much from Charlie since he probably won't fulfill their expectations.
Ⓓ They expect Charlie to do all the work around the house while earning straight A's.

2. Part A
What does this excerpt reveal about Charlie?

Ⓐ Charlie did not ask his mother for help with his clothes.
Ⓑ Charlie did not listen carefully to his mother's instructions on how to wash his clothes.
Ⓒ Charlie tried to enjoy doing his laundry.
Ⓓ Charlie is so eager to get his homework completed on time that he forgets the laundry instructions.

Part B
After Charlie had a mishap with his laundry, he laughed. What does this reveal about Charlie's character?

Ⓐ Charlie is the kind of person who realizes what's done is done; all he can do is try again.
Ⓑ Charlie is the kind of person who laughs wildly when he isn't sure how to react to stressful situations.
Ⓒ Charlie is the kind of person who laughs at the misfortune of others.
Ⓓ Charlie is the kind of person who laughs when he isn't sure what to do.

Question 3-5 are based on the story below

Excerpt from **Stave Five of A Christmas Carol** by Charles Dickens

(1) "What else can I be," returned the uncle [Scrooge], "when I live in such a world of fools as this? Merry Christmas! Out upon Merry Christmas! What's Christmas time to you but a time for paying bills without money; a time for finding yourself a year older, but not an hour richer; a time for balancing your books and having every item in 'em through a round dozen of months presented dead against you? If I could work my will," said Scrooge indignantly, "every idiot who goes about with 'Merry Christmas' on his lips should be boiled with his own pudding, and buried with a stake of holly through his heart. He should!"

Excerpt from **Stave Five of A Christmas Carol** by Charles Dickens

(2) "A merry Christmas, Bob!" said Scrooge [the uncle], with an earnestness that could not be mistaken, as he clapped him on the back. "A merrier Christmas, Bob, my good fellow, than I have given you, for many a year! I'll raise your salary, and endeavor to assist your struggling family, and we will discuss your affairs this very afternoon, over a Christmas bowl of smoking bishop, Bob! Make up the fires, and buy another coal-scuttle before you dot another, Bob Cratchit!"

3. What is the significance of this dialogue from both excerpts?

Ⓐ This dialogue is significant because it shows that Scrooge wants to wish the person he's addressing a Merry Christmas.
Ⓑ This dialogue is significant because it is important for the reader to know Scrooge's feelings about Christmas.
Ⓒ This dialogue is significant because Scrooge wants to make sure everyone knows he dislikes Christmas.
Ⓓ This dialogue is significant because it shows Scrooge cannot wait for Christmas morning to come, so he can rip open his presents.

4. What is the most important purpose of this dialogue?

Ⓐ It allows the reader to really understand the change that Scrooge underwent in the story.
Ⓑ It allows the reader to see that Scrooge liked Christmas all along.
Ⓒ It allows the reader to see that nothing could change Scrooge's opinion of Christmas.
Ⓓ None of the above

5. Why is it important to understand what characters can reveal to readers?

Ⓐ It allows readers to see and understand how characters interact with the setting.
Ⓑ It allows readers to see and understand how characters interact with other characters.
Ⓒ It allows readers to see and understand how the actions of a character can drive the plot.
Ⓓ All of the above

Question 6 and 7 are based on the passage below

Casey Jones-A Tennessee Legend
-retold by S.E. Schlosser

Casey Jones, that heroic railroad engineer of the Cannonball, was known as the man who always brought the train in on time. He would blow the whistle, so it started off soft but would increase to a wail louder than a banshee before dying off so that people would recognize that whistle and know when Casey was driving past.

April 29, 1900, Casey brought the Cannonball into Memphis dead on time. As he was leaving, he found out one of the other engineers was sick and unable to make his run. So Casey volunteered to help out his friend. He pulled the train out of the station about eleven p.m., an hour and thirty-five minutes late. Casey was determined to make up the time. As soon as he could, he highballed out of Memphis (highballing means to go very fast and take a lot of risks to get where you are headed) and started making up for the lost time.

About four a.m., when he had nearly made up all the time on the run, Casey rounded a corner near Vaughn, Mississippi, and saw a stalled freight train on the track. He shouted for his fireman to jump. The fireman made it out alive, but Casey Jones died in the wreck, one hand on the brake and one on the whistle chord.

6. Which of the statements below best describes Casey Jones?

  Ⓐ He was a large hearted, friendly man known to most as the Cannonball.
  Ⓑ He was a large hearted, courageous, and punctual man.
  Ⓒ He was so concerned about being punctual, he was not careful when driving.
  Ⓓ None of the above

7. What do Casey's actions in the last paragraph reveal about him?

  Ⓐ He wasn't very smart because he didn't jump off the train in time.
  Ⓑ He did not care for his firemen.
  Ⓒ Up to his very last act, he was courageous.
  Ⓓ None of the above

Question 8 is based on the passage below

The Grasshopper and the Ants-Aesop's Fable

In a field, one summer's day, a grasshopper was hopping about, chirping and singing to its heart's content. A group of ants walked by, grunting as they struggled to carry plump kernels of corn. "Where are you going with those heavy things?" asked the grasshopper. Without stopping, the first ant replied, "To our anthill. This is the third kernel I've delivered today."

"Why not come and sing with me," teased the grasshopper, "instead of working so hard?"

"We are helping to store food for the winter," said the ant, "and think you should do the same."

"Winter is far away, and it is a glorious day to play," sang the grasshopper. But the ants went on their way and continued their hard work.

The weather soon turned cold. All the food lying in the field was covered with a thick white blanket of snow that even the grasshopper could not dig through.

Soon the grasshopper found itself dying of hunger. He staggered to the ants' hill and saw them handing out corn from the stores they had collected in the summer. He begged them for something to eat.

"What!" cried the ants in surprise, "haven't you stored anything away for the winter? What in the world were you doing all last summer?"

"I didn't have time to store any food," complained the grasshopper; "I was so busy playing music that before I knew, it the summer was gone."

The ants shook their heads in disgust, turned their backs on the grasshopper, and went on with their work.

8. Part A
What does the response of the first ant to the grasshopper reveal for readers?

Ⓐ He is taking his work seriously.
Ⓑ He doesn't like grasshoppers.
Ⓒ He likes to work alone.
Ⓓ He has just started working and doesn't want to be bothered.

Part B
What does the grasshopper's response to the ant reveal about the grasshopper?

Ⓐ He is trying to be responsible.
Ⓑ He is afraid of the ant.
Ⓒ He is not very responsible.
Ⓓ He is very similar to the ant.

Part C
What do the ants' response to the grasshopper reveal about the ants' opinion of the grasshopper's attitude?

Ⓐ They are proud of what the grasshopper has done.
Ⓑ They want to become friendlier with the grasshopper.
Ⓒ They are unsure of what to say to the grasshopper.
Ⓓ They can't believe the grasshopper would be so careless.

Test ID	8E009
Test Name	**Meaning and Tone**
Student Name	
Date	

1	Ⓐ Ⓑ Ⓒ Ⓓ	6	Ⓐ Ⓑ Ⓒ Ⓓ	10 B	Ⓐ Ⓑ Ⓒ Ⓓ
2	Ⓐ Ⓑ Ⓒ Ⓓ	7	Ⓐ Ⓑ Ⓒ Ⓓ	11	Answer in the space provided below.
3	Ⓐ Ⓑ Ⓒ Ⓓ	8	Ⓐ Ⓑ Ⓒ Ⓓ	12	Answer in the space provided below.
4	Ⓐ Ⓑ Ⓒ Ⓓ	9	Ⓐ Ⓑ Ⓒ Ⓓ		
5	Ⓐ Ⓑ Ⓒ Ⓓ	10 A	Ⓐ Ⓑ Ⓒ Ⓓ		

11

12

Chapter 1 → Lesson 9: Meaning and Tone

1. What is the tone of a piece of literature?

- Ⓐ the rhythm of the words when read out loud
- Ⓑ the level of sound with which it should be read
- Ⓒ the author's attitude about the subject and/or the readers
- Ⓓ none of the above

2. What is the tone of this sentence?

Tonight's homework is to read thirty pages in the textbook.

- Ⓐ neutral
- Ⓑ dramatic
- Ⓒ angry
- Ⓓ friendly

3. What is the tone of the below sentence?

Oh great! My thoughtful teacher gave us homework again tonight! Sure, I have nothing better to do than read thirty pages out of an outdated textbook. I don't have a life.

- Ⓐ expectant
- Ⓑ sad
- Ⓒ sarcastic
- Ⓓ adoring

4. What is the tone of the below sentence?

I simply cannot believe that after all the reading we have done this week, we have to read thirty pages tonight. This is an outrage!

- Ⓐ angry
- Ⓑ gleeful
- Ⓒ skeptical
- Ⓓ questioning

Excerpt from Because of Winn-Dixie
by Kate DiCamillo

The Open Arms had mice. They were there from when it was a Pick-It-Quick and there were lots of good things to eat in the building, and when the Pick-It-Quick became the Open Arms Baptist Church of Naomi, the mice stayed around to eat all the leftover crumbs from the potluck suppers. The preacher kept on saying he was going to have to do something about them, but he never did. Because the truth is, he couldn't stand the thought of hurting anything, even a mouse.

Well, Winn-Dixie saw that mouse, and he was up and after him. One minute, everything was quiet and serious and the preacher was going on and on and on; and the next minute, Winn-Dixie looked like a furry bullet, shooting across the building, chasing that mouse. He was barking and his feet were skidding all over the polished Pick-It-Quick floor, and people were clapping and hollering and pointing. They really went wild when Winn-Dixie actually caught the mouse.

5. What is the tone in this excerpt?

- Ⓐ romantic
- Ⓑ unemotional
- Ⓒ enthusiastic
- Ⓓ morose

From **Narrative of the Life of Frederick Douglass, an American Slave**

This battle with Mr. Covey was the turning point in my career as a slave. It rekindled the few expiring embers of freedom, and revived within me a sense of my own manhood.

6. What is the tone of the statement above?

- Ⓐ encouraging
- Ⓑ sarcastic
- Ⓒ unemotional
- Ⓓ sorrowful

Excerpt from **"The Story of the Wild Huntsman"** by Heinrich Hoffmann

This is the Wild Huntsman that shoots the hares
With the grass-green coat he always wears:
With game-bag, powder-horn and gun,
He's going out to have some fun.
He finds it hard, without a pair
Of spectacles, to shoot the hare:
He put his spectacles upon his nose, and said,
"Now I will shoot the hares, and kill them dead."
The hare sits snug in leaves and grass
And laughs to see the green man pass

7. What is the tone of this excerpt?

Ⓐ   joyous
Ⓑ   formal
Ⓒ   serious
Ⓓ   comical

8. In this sentence, what does "snug" most likely mean?

Ⓐ   seaworthiness
Ⓑ   fitting closely
Ⓒ   privacy
Ⓓ   humorous

9. In this excerpt, what does "spectacles" most likely means?

Ⓐ   something unusual
Ⓑ   something one would be curious about
Ⓒ   dramatic display
Ⓓ   glasses

Question 10 is based on the passage below

The Ungrateful Son
By Jacob and Wilhelm Grimm

Once a man was sitting with his wife before their front door. They had a roasted chicken which they were about to eat together. Then the man saw that his aged father was approaching, and he hastily took the chicken and hid it, for he did not want to share it with him. The old man came, had a drink, and went away. Now the son wanted to put the roasted chicken back onto the table, but when he reached for it, it had turned into a large toad, which jumped into his face and sat there and never went away again. If anyone tried to remove it, it looked venomously at him as though it would jump into his face, so that no one dared to touch it. And the ungrateful son was forced to feed the toad every day, or else it would eat from his face. And thus he went to and fro in the world without rest.

10. Part A
In this story, what does "hastily" most likely mean?

Ⓐ hurriedly
Ⓑ slowly
Ⓒ carefully
Ⓓ quietly

Part B
In this story, "venomously" most closely means

Ⓐ poisonous
Ⓑ acting like a snake
Ⓒ showing strong anger
Ⓓ striking

Question 11 and 12 are based on the passage below

Once upon a midnight dreary, while I pondered, weak and weary,
Over many a quaint and curious volume of forgotten lore,
While I nodded, nearly napping, suddenly there came a tapping,
As of some one gently rapping, rapping at my chamber door.
''Tis some visitor,' I muttered, 'tapping at my chamber door-
Only this, and nothing more.'

Ah, distinctly I remember it was in the bleak December,
And each separate dying ember wrought its ghost upon the floor.
Eagerly I wished the morrow;- vainly I had sought to borrow
From my books surcease of sorrow- sorrow for the lost Lenore-

For the rare and radiant maiden whom the angels name Lenore-
Nameless here for evermore.

And the silken sad uncertain rustling of each purple curtain
Thrilled me- filled me with fantastic terrors never felt before;
So that now, to still the beating of my heart, I stood repeating,
''Tis some visitor entreating entrance at my chamber door-
Some late visitor entreating entrance at my chamber door;-
This it is, and nothing more.'

Presently my soul grew stronger; hesitating then no longer,
'Sir,' said I, 'or Madam, truly your forgiveness I implore;
But the fact is I was napping, and so gently you came rapping,
And so faintly you came tapping, tapping at my chamber door,
That I scarce was sure I heard you'- here I opened wide the door;-
Darkness there, and nothing more.

Deep into that darkness peering, long I stood there wondering,
fearing,
Doubting, dreaming dreams no mortals ever dared to dream before;
But the silence was unbroken, and the stillness gave no token,
And the only word there spoken was the whispered word, 'Lenore!'
This I whispered, and an echo murmured back the word, 'Lenore!'-
Merely this, and nothing more.

Back into the chamber turning, all my soul within me burning,
Soon again I heard a tapping somewhat louder than before.
'Surely,' said I, 'surely that is something at my window lattice:
Let me see, then, what thereat is, and this mystery explore-
Let my heart be still a moment and this mystery explore;-
'Tis the wind and nothing more.'

Open here I flung the shutter, when, with many a flirt and
flutter,
In there stepped a stately raven of the saintly days of yore;
Not the least obeisance made he; not a minute stopped or stayed
he;
But, with mien of lord or lady, perched above my chamber door-
Perched upon a bust of Pallas just above my chamber door-
Perched, and sat, and nothing more.

Then this ebony bird beguiling my sad fancy into smiling,

By the grave and stern decorum of the countenance it wore.
'Though thy crest be shorn and shaven, thou,' I said, 'art sure no craven,
Ghastly grim and ancient raven wandering from the Nightly shore-
Tell me what thy lordly name is on the Night's Plutonian shore!'
Quoth the Raven, 'Nevermore.'

Much I marvelled this ungainly fowl to hear discourse so plainly,
Though its answer little meaning- little relevancy bore;
For we cannot help agreeing that no living human being
Ever yet was blest with seeing bird above his chamber door-
Bird or beast upon the sculptured bust above his chamber door,
With such name as 'Nevermore.'

But the raven, sitting lonely on the placid bust, spoke only
That one word, as if his soul in that one word he did outpour.
Nothing further then he uttered- not a feather then he fluttered-
Till I scarcely more than muttered, 'other friends have flown before-
On the morrow he will leave me, as my hopes have flown before.'
Then the bird said, 'Nevermore.'

Startled at the stillness broken by reply so aptly spoken,
'Doubtless,' said I, 'what it utters is its only stock and store,
Caught from some unhappy master whom unmerciful Disaster
Followed fast and followed faster till his songs one burden bore-
Till the dirges of his Hope that melancholy burden bore
Of 'Never- nevermore'.'

But the Raven still beguiling all my fancy into smiling,
Straight I wheeled a cushioned seat in front of bird, and bust and door;
Then upon the velvet sinking, I betook myself to linking
Fancy unto fancy, thinking what this ominous bird of yore-
What this grim, ungainly, ghastly, gaunt and ominous bird of yore
Meant in croaking 'Nevermore.'

This I sat engaged in guessing, but no syllable expressing
To the fowl whose fiery eyes now burned into my bosom's core;
This and more I sat divining, with my head at ease reclining
On the cushion's velvet lining that the lamplight gloated o'er,
But whose velvet violet lining with the lamplight gloating o'er,
She shall press, ah, nevermore!

Then methought the air grew denser, perfumed from an unseen censer
Swung by Seraphim whose footfalls tinkled on the tufted floor.
'Wretch,' I cried, 'thy God hath lent thee- by these angels he
hath sent thee
Respite- respite and nepenthe, from thy memories of Lenore!
Quaff, oh quaff this kind nepenthe and forget this lost Lenore!'
Quoth the Raven, 'Nevermore.'

'Prophet!' said I, 'thing of evil!- prophet still, if bird or
devil!-
Whether Tempter sent, or whether tempest tossed thee here ashore,
Desolate yet all undaunted, on this desert land enchanted-
On this home by horror haunted- tell me truly, I implore-
Is there- is there balm in Gilead?- tell me- tell me, I implore!'
Quoth the Raven, 'Nevermore.'

'Prophet!' said I, 'thing of evil- prophet still, if bird or
devil!
By that Heaven that bends above us- by that God we both adore-
Tell this soul with sorrow laden if, within the distant Aidenn,
It shall clasp a sainted maiden whom the angels name Lenore-
Clasp a rare and radiant maiden whom the angels name Lenore.'
Quoth the Raven, 'Nevermore.'

'Be that word our sign in parting, bird or fiend,' I shrieked,
upstarting-
'Get thee back into the tempest and the Night's Plutonian shore!
Leave no black plume as a token of that lie thy soul hath spoken!
Leave my loneliness unbroken!- quit the bust above my door!
Take thy beak from out my heart, and take thy form from off my
door!'
Quoth the Raven, 'Nevermore.'

And the Raven, never flitting, still is sitting, still is sitting
On the pallid bust of Pallas just above my chamber door;
And his eyes have all the seeming of a demon's that is dreaming,
And the lamplight o'er him streaming throws his shadow on the
floor;
And my soul from out that shadow that lies floating on the floor
Shall be lifted- nevermore!

Synopsis of THE RAVEN

The poem is set on a dreary night while the narrator is reading by a dying fire in attempts to forget his love, Lenore's death. He hears a tapping at his door and finds nothing. The tap then gets louder. The narrator realizes it is coming from a window. When he opens the window, a raven flies in and sits above the door.

He is then sort of interested and amused by the bird. He asks the bird what his name is, but the raven only says, "Nevermore". This surprises the narrator that the bird can talk. He says the bird will fly out of his life like others have. The bird again says, "Nevermore" leading the narrator to think he has had a cruel master. He thinks that is the only word the bird knows.

The narrator is curious to see what the raven will do and pulls up a chair directly in front of him. He wants to learn more about the bird. He lets his mind wander to his lost love Lenore. He feels the presence of angels and now believes this could be a sign from God. When he asks the bird, the raven replies the negative comment again. Now the narrator becomes angry and feels the raven is a devil or evil bird. The word, "Nevermore" is again repeated. The man is outraged and tells the bird to leave. It does not. The narrator falls into a deep state of depression.

11. **Why do you think the raven was chosen to be used in this poem? Write your answer in the box below.**

12. **The narrator in the poem thinks that the raven could have been sent by two different forces. What are they? Write your answer in the box below.**

Test ID	8E010
Test Name	**Compare and Contrast**
Student Name	
Date	

1	Ⓐ Ⓑ Ⓒ Ⓓ	6	Ⓐ Ⓑ Ⓒ Ⓓ	10	Answer in the space provided below.
2	Ⓐ Ⓑ Ⓒ Ⓓ	7	Ⓐ Ⓑ Ⓒ Ⓓ		
3	Ⓐ Ⓑ Ⓒ Ⓓ	8 A	Ⓐ Ⓑ Ⓒ Ⓓ		
4	Ⓐ Ⓑ Ⓒ Ⓓ	8 B	Ⓐ Ⓑ Ⓒ Ⓓ		
5	Ⓐ Ⓑ Ⓒ Ⓓ	9	Ⓐ Ⓑ Ⓒ Ⓓ		

10
×

+

Chapter 1 → Lesson 10: Compare and Contrast

1. When you are comparing two things, what are you looking for?

- Ⓐ similarities
- Ⓑ differences
- Ⓒ similarities and differences
- Ⓓ none of the above

2. Which of the following group of signal words would you most likely find in a paper comparing two things?

- Ⓐ in addition, finally, above all
- Ⓑ meanwhile, coupled with, for instance
- Ⓒ likewise, as well, the same as
- Ⓓ although, however, contrary to

3. Which of the following graphic organizers is most effectively used to compare and contrast?

- Ⓐ Venn diagram
- Ⓑ Brace map
- Ⓒ Fish bone map
- Ⓓ Tree map

4. When you are contrasting two things, what are you looking for?

- Ⓐ similarities
- Ⓑ differences
- Ⓒ similarities and differences
- Ⓓ none of the above

5. In a Venn diagram, where does the "common" information belong?

- Ⓐ in the middle
- Ⓑ on the right
- Ⓒ on the left
- Ⓓ no where

6. Which of the following group of signal words would you most likely find in a paper contrasting two things?

- Ⓐ in addition, finally, above all
- Ⓑ meanwhile, coupled with, for instance
- Ⓒ likewise, as well, the same as
- Ⓓ although, however, contrary to

Question 7 and 8 are based on the poems below

The Mountain and The Squirrel	The Arrow and the Song
The mountain and the squirrel Had a quarrel; And the former called the latter, "Little Prig." Bun replied "You are doubtless very big; But all sorts of things and weather Must be taken in together To make up a year And a sphere. And I think it no disgrace To occupy my place. If I'm not so large as you, You are not so small as I, And not half so spry; I'll not deny you make A very pretty squirrel track; Talents differ; all is well and wisely put; If I cannot carry forests on my back, Neither can you crack a nut" **Ralph Waldo Emerson** (1803 - 1882)	I shot an arrow into the air It fell to earth, I knew not where; For, so swiftly it flew, the sight Could not follow it in its flight. I breathed a song into the air It fell to earth, I knew not where For who has sight so keen and strong That it can follow the flight of song? Long, long afterward, in an oak I found the arrow, still unbroke And the song, from beginning to end I found again in the heart of a friend. **H. W. Longfellow** (1807 - 1882)

7. Both poems share a similar setting which is _____.

   Ⓐ nature
   Ⓑ the mountains
   Ⓒ a lake
   Ⓓ a tree

8. Part A
What is one comparison the reader can make about both poems?

   Ⓐ Both the poems were written during the 19th century.
   Ⓑ One of the poems was written in the 20th century.
   Ⓒ Both the poems were written in the 20th century.
   Ⓓ One of the poems was written in the 19th century.

8. Part B

A difference between the poems is _____.

Ⓐ dialogue
Ⓑ point of view
Ⓒ both A & B
Ⓓ none of the above

Question 9 is based on the passage below

Henry Wordsworth Longfellow was an American poet who lived from 1807 to 1882. Longfellow was born and raised in the region of Portland, Maine. Longfellow was enrolled in dame school at the age of only three. By age six, when he entered Portland Academy, he was able to read and write quite well. He graduated from Bowdoin College in Brunswick, Maine, in 1822. At Bowdoin, he met Nathaniel Hawthorne, who became his lifelong friend. After several journeys overseas, Longfellow settled for the last forty-five years of his life in Cambridge, Massachusetts. Longfellow was one of the five members of the group known as the Fireside Poets. During his years at the college, he wrote textbooks in French, Italian, and Spanish and a travel book, Outre-mer: A Pilgrimage Beyond the Sea Longfellow was such an admired figure in the United States during his life that his 70th birthday in 1877 took on the air of a national holiday, with parades, speeches, and the reading of his poetry. He had become one of the first American celebrities. His work was immensely popular during his time and is still today, although some modern critics consider him too sentimental. His poetry is based on familiar and easily understood themes with simple, clear, and flowing language. His poetry created an audience in America and contributed to creating American mythology.

Ralph Waldo Emerson was an American essayist, poet, and leader of the trancendentalist movement in the early 19th century. He was born and brought up in Boston, Massachusetts. Emerson lost his father at the age of 8 and was subsequently sent to Boston Latin School at the age of 9. He went to Harvard College at the age of 14 and graduated in 1821. Emerson made his living as a schoolmaster and then went to Harvard Divinity School and emerged as a Unitarian Minister in 1829. A dispute with church officials over the administration of the Communion service and misgivings about public prayer led to his resignation in 1832. In the 1840's Emerson was hospitable to Nathanial Hawthorne and his family, influencing Hawthorne during his three joyous years with Emerson. Emerson was noted as being a very abstract and difficult writer who nevertheless drew large crowds for his speeches. The heart of Emerson's writing were his direct observations in his hournals, which he started keeping as a teenager at Harvard. Emerson has written a lot of essays on, History, Self-reliance, love, friendship, heroism etc... He died in 1882 and is buried in the sleepy hollow Cemetery, Concord, Massachusetts. His house, which he bought in 1835 in Concord, Massachusetts, is now open to the public as the Ralph Waldo Emerson house.

9. According to the above passages, what is common between the above writers?

Ⓐ Both the writers were born in America.
Ⓑ Both the writers lived at the same time (19th Century).
Ⓒ Both the writers were associated with Nathaniel Hawthorne.
Ⓓ All of the above.

Question 10 is based on the poem below

The Raven

Once upon a midnight dreary, while I pondered, weak and weary,
Over many a quaint and curious volume of forgotten lore,
While I nodded, nearly napping, suddenly there came a tapping,
As of some one gently rapping, rapping at my chamber door.
''Tis some visitor,' I muttered, 'tapping at my chamber door-
Only this, and nothing more.'

Ah, distinctly I remember it was in the bleak December,
And each separate dying ember wrought its ghost upon the floor.
Eagerly I wished the morrow;- vainly I had sought to borrow
From my books surcease of sorrow- sorrow for the lost Lenore-
For the rare and radiant maiden whom the angels name Lenore-
Nameless here for evermore.

And the silken sad uncertain rustling of each purple curtain
Thrilled me- filled me with fantastic terrors never felt before;
So that now, to still the beating of my heart, I stood repeating,
''Tis some visitor entreating entrance at my chamber door-
Some late visitor entreating entrance at my chamber door;-
This it is, and nothing more.'

Presently my soul grew stronger; hesitating then no longer,
'Sir,' said I, 'or Madam, truly your forgiveness I implore;
But the fact is I was napping, and so gently you came rapping,
And so faintly you came tapping, tapping at my chamber door,
That I scarce was sure I heard you'- here I opened wide the door;-
Darkness there, and nothing more.

Deep into that darkness peering, long I stood there wondering, fearing,
Doubting, dreaming dreams no mortals ever dared to dream before;
But the silence was unbroken, and the stillness gave no token,
And the only word there spoken was the whispered word, 'Lenore!'

This I whispered, and an echo murmured back the word, 'Lenore!'-
Merely this, and nothing more.

Back into the chamber turning, all my soul within me burning,
Soon again I heard a tapping somewhat louder than before.
'Surely,' said I, 'surely that is something at my window lattice:
Let me see, then, what thereat is, and this mystery explore-
Let my heart be still a moment and this mystery explore;-
'Tis the wind and nothing more.'

Open here I flung the shutter, when, with many a flirt and flutter,
In there stepped a stately raven of the saintly days of yore;
Not the least obeisance made he; not a minute stopped or stayed he;
But, with mien of lord or lady, perched above my chamber door-
Perched upon a bust of Pallas just above my chamber door-
Perched, and sat, and nothing more.

Then this ebony bird beguiling my sad fancy into smiling,
By the grave and stern decorum of the countenance it wore.
'Though thy crest be shorn and shaven, thou,' I said, 'art sure no craven,
Ghastly grim and ancient raven wandering from the Nightly shore-
Tell me what thy lordly name is on the Night's Plutonian shore!'
Quoth the Raven, 'Nevermore.'

Much I marvelled this ungainly fowl to hear discourse so plainly,
Though its answer little meaning- little relevancy bore;
For we cannot help agreeing that no living human being
Ever yet was blest with seeing bird above his chamber door-
Bird or beast upon the sculptured bust above his chamber door,
With such name as 'Nevermore.'

But the raven, sitting lonely on the placid bust, spoke only
That one word, as if his soul in that one word he did outpour.
Nothing further then he uttered- not a feather then he fluttered-
Till I scarcely more than muttered, 'other friends have flown before-
On the morrow he will leave me, as my hopes have flown before.'
Then the bird said, 'Nevermore.'

Startled at the stillness broken by reply so aptly spoken,
'Doubtless,' said I, 'what it utters is its only stock and store,
Caught from some unhappy master whom unmerciful Disaster
Followed fast and followed faster till his songs one burden bore-
Till the dirges of his Hope that melancholy burden bore
Of 'Never- nevermore'.'

But the Raven still beguiling all my fancy into smiling,
Straight I wheeled a cushioned seat in front of bird, and bust and door;
Then upon the velvet sinking, I betook myself to linking
Fancy unto fancy, thinking what this ominous bird of yore-
What this grim, ungainly, ghastly, gaunt and ominous bird of yore
Meant in croaking 'Nevermore.'

This I sat engaged in guessing, but no syllable expressing
To the fowl whose fiery eyes now burned into my bosom's core;
This and more I sat divining, with my head at ease reclining
On the cushion's velvet lining that the lamplight gloated o'er,
But whose velvet violet lining with the lamplight gloating o'er,
She shall press, ah, nevermore!

Then methought the air grew denser, perfumed from an unseen censer
Swung by Seraphim whose footfalls tinkled on the tufted floor.
'Wretch,' I cried, 'thy God hath lent thee- by these angels he hath sent thee
Respite- respite and nepenthe, from thy memories of Lenore!
Quaff, oh quaff this kind nepenthe and forget this lost Lenore!'
Quoth the Raven, 'Nevermore.'

'Prophet!' said I, 'thing of evil!- prophet still, if bird or devil!-
Whether Tempter sent, or whether tempest tossed thee here ashore,
Desolate yet all undaunted, on this desert land enchanted-
On this home by horror haunted- tell me truly, I implore-
Is there- is there balm in Gilead?- tell me- tell me, I implore!'
Quoth the Raven, 'Nevermore.'

'Prophet!' said I, 'thing of evil- prophet still, if bird or devil!
By that Heaven that bends above us- by that God we both adore-
Tell this soul with sorrow laden if, within the distant Aidenn,
It shall clasp a sainted maiden whom the angels name Lenore-
Clasp a rare and radiant maiden whom the angels name Lenore.'
Quoth the Raven, 'Nevermore.'

'Be that word our sign in parting, bird or fiend,' I shrieked, upstarting-
'Get thee back into the tempest and the Night's Plutonian shore!
Leave no black plume as a token of that lie thy soul hath spoken!
Leave my loneliness unbroken!- quit the bust above my door!
Take thy beak from out my heart, and take thy form from off my door!'
Quoth the Raven, 'Nevermore.'

And the Raven, never flitting, still is sitting, still is sitting
On the pallid bust of Pallas just above my chamber door;
And his eyes have all the seeming of a demon's that is dreaming,
And the lamplight o'er him streaming throws his shadow on the floor;
And my soul from out that shadow that lies floating on the floor
Shall be lifted- nevermore!

Synopsis of THE RAVEN

The poem is set on a dreary night while the narrator is reading by a dying fire in attempts to forget his love, Lenore's death. He hears a tapping at his door and finds nothing. The tap then gets louder. The narrator realizes it is coming from a window. When he opens the window, a raven flies in and sits above the door.

He is then sort of interested and amuse by the bird. He asks the bird what his name is, but the raven only says, "Nevermore". This surprises the narrator that the bird can talk. He says the bird will fly out of his life like others have. The bird again says, "Nevermore" leading the narrator to think he has had a cruel master. He thinks that is the only word the bird knows.

The narrator is curious to see what the raven will do and pulls up a chair directly in front of him. He wants to learn more about the bird. He lets his mind wander to his lost love Lenore. He feels the presence of angels and now believes this could be a sign from God. When he asks the bird, the raven replies the negative comment again. Now the narrator becomes angry and feels the raven is a devil or evil bird. The word, "Nevermore" is again repeated. The man is outraged and tells the bird to leave. It does not. The narrator falls into a deep state of depression.

10. Did the synopsis help you to understand the poem better? Explain your answer. Write your answer in the box below.

Test ID	8E011
Test Name	**Producing Suspense and Humor**
Student Name	
Date	

1	(A) (B) (C) (D)	6	(A) (B) (C) (D)	11	Answer in the space provided below.
2	(A) (B) (C) (D)	7	(A) (B) (C) (D)	12	Answer in the space provided below.
3	(A) (B) (C) (D)	8	(A) (B) (C) (D)		
4	(A) (B) (C) (D)	9	(A) (B) (C) (D)		
5	(A) (B) (C) (D)	10	(A) (B) (C) (D)		

11

12

Chapter 1 → Lesson 11: Producing Suspense and Humor

1. Which of the following is an example of a pun?

Ⓐ A boiled egg every morning is hard to beat.
Ⓑ Nicholas went to buy some camouflage pants the other day, but he couldn't find any.
Ⓒ Our social studies teacher says her globe means the world to her.
Ⓓ all of the above

2. What literary elements can add humor to a story?

Ⓐ pun
Ⓑ setting or situation
Ⓒ irony
Ⓓ all of the above

3. What is the best definition of irony?

Ⓐ interesting dialogue between characters
Ⓑ a scene in which something is complex and difficult to understand
Ⓒ surprising, funny, or interesting contradictions
Ⓓ a line that is straight to the point

Question 4 is based on the poem below

Excerpt from **The Story of the Wild Huntsman** by Heinrich Hoffmann

This is the Wild Huntsman that shoots the hares
With the grass-green coat he always wears:
With game-bag, powder-horn and gun,
He's going out to have some fun.
He finds it hard, without a pair
Of spectacles, to shoot the hare:
He put his spectacles upon his nose, and said,
"Now I will shoot the hares, and kill them dead."
The hare sits snug in leaves and grass
And laughs to see the green man pass

4. The author creates humor through his description of _____.

Ⓐ the laughing rabbit
Ⓑ the hunter who is excited to kill a rabbit
Ⓒ the hunter who is over-prepared to hunt
Ⓓ the description of the spectacle

Question 5 is based on the paragraph below

It was a cold and windy evening. The clouds had a haunting presence in the sky. Cindy walked briskly down the street, conscious of the quiet around her. As she approached her front door, she noticed something wasn't right. There was a light on inside, and she thought she could hear someone running down the stairs. Her husband, however, wasn't due home for a couple of hours.

5. This description builds a sense of _____.

(A) irony
(B) suspense
(C) humor
(D) confusion

Question 6 is based on the paragraph below

In the story *Romeo and Juliet* by William Shakespeare, Romeo commits suicide because he thinks that Juliet is dead. However, the reader knows that she is just in a deep sleep because she took a potion that made her appear dead.

6. What type of irony does Shakespeare use?

(A) dramatic irony
(B) verbal irony
(C) situational irony
(D) none of the above

Question 7 is based on the paragraph below

A man wakes up early to wash his car before a trip to the park to watch a baseball game. After the game, he realizes that he parked under a tree filled with birds and now his car is covered in white splattered patches. The man said with a loud sigh, "Gee, I sure am glad I woke up early to wash my car."

7. What type of irony does the author use?

(A) dramatic irony
(B) verbal irony
(C) situational irony
(D) none of the above

Question 8 is based on the paragraph below

During a ceremony to release two rehabilitated seals into the ocean, the seals are attacked and killed by whales.

8. What type of irony does the author use?

Ⓐ dramatic irony
Ⓑ verbal irony
Ⓒ situational irony
Ⓓ none of the above

Question 9 is based on the paragraph below

Caitlin saved for years to be able to afford her dream vacation to Tahiti. The morning of her flight she received a phone call from a talk show. If she answered the question correctly she would win a vacation. To her surprise, she answered the question correctly, and the host announced she had won an all-expense paid vacation to Tahiti.

9. What type of irony does the author use?

Ⓐ situational irony
Ⓑ verbal irony
Ⓒ dramatic irony
Ⓓ all of the above

Question 10 is based on the paragraph below

Kyle knew he needed to study for his biology test, but he was so close to beating the next level of his video game that he just couldn't tear himself away from the screen. An hour later, his mom came into his room and said, "Kyle, when you are finished the very important task of beating this level, why don't you consider opening up your binder and studying for your biology test?"

10. What type of irony does the author use?

Ⓐ situational irony
Ⓑ verbal irony
Ⓒ dramatic irony
Ⓓ building suspense

The Tempest, Act III, Scene II [Be not afeard]

William Shakespeare, 1564 - 1616

Caliban speaks to Stephano and Trinculo.

Be not afeard; the isle is full of noises,
Sounds and sweet airs, that give delight, and hurt not.
Sometimes a thousand twangling instruments
Will hum about mine ears; and sometime voices,
That, if I then had waked after long sleep,
Will make me sleep again: and then, in dreaming,
The clouds methought would open, and show riches
Ready to drop upon me; that, when I waked,
I cried to dream again.

11. Describe what not to be afraid of? Write your answer in the box below.

12. Why did he want to dream again? Write your answer in the box below.

Test ID	8E012
Test Name	**Media and Literature**
Student Name	
Date	

1	Ⓐ Ⓑ Ⓒ Ⓓ	6	Ⓐ Ⓑ Ⓒ Ⓓ
2	Ⓐ Ⓑ Ⓒ Ⓓ	7 A	Ⓐ Ⓑ Ⓒ Ⓓ
3	Ⓐ Ⓑ Ⓒ Ⓓ	7 B	Ⓐ Ⓑ Ⓒ Ⓓ
4	Ⓐ Ⓑ Ⓒ Ⓓ	8 A	Ⓐ Ⓑ Ⓒ Ⓓ
5	Ⓐ Ⓑ Ⓒ Ⓓ	8 B	Ⓐ Ⓑ Ⓒ Ⓓ

Chapter 1 → Lesson 12: Media and Literature

Question 1-3 are based on the paragraph below

Casey Jones-A Tennessee Legend
-retold by S.E. Schlosser

Casey Jones, that heroic railroad engineer of the Cannonball, was known as the man who always brought the train in on time. He would blow the whistle, so it started off soft but would increase to a wail louder than a banshee before dying off so that people would recognize that whistle and know when Casey was driving past.

April 29, 1900, Casey brought the Cannonball into Memphis dead on time. As he was leaving, he found out one of the other engineers was sick and unable to make his run. So Casey volunteered to help out his friend. He pulled the train out of the station about eleven p.m., an hour and thirty-five minutes late. Casey was determined to make up the time. As soon as he could, he highballed out of Memphis (highballing means to go very fast and take a lot of risks to get where you are headed) and started making up for the lost time.

About four a.m., when he had nearly made up all the time on the run, Casey rounded a corner near Vaughn, Mississippi, and saw a stalled freight train on the track. He shouted for his fireman to jump. The fireman made it out alive, but Casey Jones died in the wreck, one hand on the brake and one on the whistle chord.

1. **What medium of publication would be best to use if you wanted to make it possible for people to see Casey Jones operating the train?**

   Ⓐ a video
   Ⓑ digital text
   Ⓒ a traditional book
   Ⓓ none of the above

2. **What are the advantages of using media to present a particular topic or idea?**

   Ⓐ It can create a picture for viewers to see
   Ⓑ It provides a clear voice for viewers to hear
   Ⓒ Both A and B
   Ⓓ None of the above

3. **If you want to see one person's visual interpretation of a character's appearance, what medium of publication would be best to use?**

   Ⓐ movie version of a text
   Ⓑ print text
   Ⓒ digital text
   Ⓓ none of the above

4. What is multimedia?

Ⓐ   A medium used to present information
Ⓑ   Using more than one medium of expression or communication.
Ⓒ   Multiple books
Ⓓ   None of the above

5. What medium of publication would be best to quickly publish your opinion about a current topic?

Ⓐ   Research paper
Ⓑ   Newspaper article
Ⓒ   Blog
Ⓓ   None of the above

6. What is the difference between an article written in a newspaper and a blog post?

Ⓐ   Newspapers are available only in printed format whereas blogs are published online.
Ⓑ   Newspaper articles are reliable resources while blogs are opinions.
Ⓒ   Blogs have to be proven true, and newspapers do not.
Ⓓ   None of the above

Question 7 and 8 are based on the poem below

The Lake Isle of Innisfree

I will arise and go now, and go to Innisfree,
And a small cabin build there, of clay and wattles made:
Nine bean-rows will I have there, a hive for the honey-bee;
And live alone in the bee-loud glade.
And I shall have some peace there, for peace comes dropping slow,
Dropping from the veils of the morning to where the cricket sings;
There midnight's all a glimmer, and noon a purple glow,
And evening full of the linnet's wings.
I will arise and go now, for always night and day
I hear lake water lapping with low sounds by the shore;
While I stand on the roadway, or on the pavements grey,
I hear it in the deep heart's core.
W. B. Yeats

About the poet:
William Butler Yeats was an Irish poet and a dramatist. He was one of the foremost figures of 20th-century literature and was the driving force behind the Irish literary revival. Together with Lady

Gregory and Edward Martin, Yeats founded the Abbey Theater. He served as its chief during its early years and was a pillar of the Irish literary establishment in his later years.

The above well-known poem explores the poet's longing for the peace and tranquility of Innisfree, a place where he spent a lot of time as a boy. This poem is a lyric.

7. **Part A**
   Which medium of publication, the poem or the picture, gives you a better visualization of the lake?

   Ⓐ the picture
   Ⓑ the poem
   Ⓒ neither
   Ⓓ both

   Part B
   Which medium of publication, the poem or the picture, appeals to more than one of the five senses?

   Ⓐ the picture
   Ⓑ the poem
   Ⓒ neither
   Ⓓ both

8. **Part A**
   Which medium of publication, the poem or the picture, is the best to visualize the lake and its surroundings?

   Ⓐ the picture
   Ⓑ the poem
   Ⓒ neither
   Ⓓ both

Part B

Which medium of publication, the poem or the picture, would be best to use on a travel brochure to attract people to the lake?

Ⓐ the picture
Ⓑ the poem
Ⓒ neither
Ⓓ both

Test ID	8E013
Test Name	**Modern Fictions and Traditional Stories**
Student Name	
Date	

1	Ⓐ Ⓑ Ⓒ Ⓓ	6	Ⓐ Ⓑ Ⓒ Ⓓ
2	Ⓐ Ⓑ Ⓒ Ⓓ	7	Ⓐ Ⓑ Ⓒ Ⓓ
3	Ⓐ Ⓑ Ⓒ Ⓓ	8	Ⓐ Ⓑ Ⓒ Ⓓ
4	Ⓐ Ⓑ Ⓒ Ⓓ	9	Ⓐ Ⓑ Ⓒ Ⓓ
5	Ⓐ Ⓑ Ⓒ Ⓓ	10	Ⓐ Ⓑ Ⓒ Ⓓ

Chapter 1 → Lesson 13: Modern Fictions and Traditional Stories

1. What is a motif?

- (A) the major characters in the story
- (B) how the story ends
- (C) the plot
- (D) a recurring element or idea in a story

2. Which of the following is/are a popular motif(s) in traditional stories?

- (A) good vs. evil
- (B) a test of courage
- (C) children who are heroes
- (D) all of the above

Question 3-5 are based on the story below

The Ant and the Grasshopper Aesop's Fable

In a field, one summer's day, a grasshopper was hopping about, chirping and singing to its heart's content. A group of ants walked by, grunting as they struggled to carry plump kernels of corn. "Where are you going with those heavy things?" asked the grasshopper.

Without stopping, the first ant replied, "To our anthill. This is the third kernel I've delivered today." "Why not come and sing with me," teased the grasshopper, "instead of working so hard?" "We are helping to store food for the winter," said the ant, "and think you should do the same." "Winter is far away, and it is a glorious day to play," sang the grasshopper. But the ants went on their way and continued their hard work.

The weather soon turned cold. All the food lying in the field was covered with a thick white blanket of snow that even the grasshopper could not dig through.

Soon the grasshopper found itself dying of hunger. He staggered to the ants' hill and saw them handing out corn from the stores they had collected in the summer. He begged them for something to eat. "What!" cried the ants in surprise, "haven't you stored anything away for the winter? What in the world were you doing all last summer?"

"I didn't have time to store any food," complained the grasshopper; "I was so busy playing music that before I knew it, the summer was gone."

The ants shook their heads in disgust, turned their backs on the grasshopper, and went on with their work.

3. **What is the lesson of this fable?**

    Ⓐ It's okay to have fun.
    Ⓑ Do not help those around you.
    Ⓒ Work hard to prepare for the future.
    Ⓓ Listen to what you are told.

4. **What type of story is "The Ant and the Grasshopper"?**

    Ⓐ a fairy tale
    Ⓑ a fable
    Ⓒ a myth
    Ⓓ folktale

5. **How does the reader know "The Ant and the Grasshopper" is a fable?**

    Ⓐ Animal characters play the role of humans.
    Ⓑ There is a moral or lesson.
    Ⓒ The story is short.
    Ⓓ all of the above

Question 6 is based on the paragraph below

There is a boy who has three brothers. His bike is broken so he goes to borrow one of his brother's. His oldest brother's bike is way too big. His younger brother's bike still has training wheels on it and is too small. His second oldest brother's bike works perfectly though, and that is the one he borrowed.

6. **What traditional story does this remind you of?**

    Ⓐ "Little Red Riding Hood"
    Ⓑ The Story of "Goldilocks and the Three Bears"
    Ⓒ "Rumpelstiltskin"
    Ⓓ "Snow White and the Seven Dwarfs"

Question 7-9 are based on the story below

You read a story about a young girl who battles against all odds to overcome the hardships of homelessness and discrimination to go to Harvard and become extremely successful.

7. What is a popular motif in this story?

Ⓐ good vs. evil
Ⓑ a test of courage
Ⓒ children who are heroes
Ⓓ true love

8. In the classic fairy tale "Cinderella," what do the characters of Cinderella and the stepmother stand for?

Ⓐ fun vs. boring
Ⓑ good vs. evil
Ⓒ young vs. old
Ⓓ traditional vs. non-traditional

9. Fill in the blank after selecting the correct answer choice from the 4 options given below.

When someone declares an event to be a "modern day Cinderella story" they mean _____.

Ⓐ someone poor or common becomes successful
Ⓑ someone has evil step-sisters
Ⓒ someone rides a carriage
Ⓓ someone is the most beautiful in her family

Casey Jones-A Tennessee Legend
-retold by S.E. Schlosser

Casey Jones, that heroic railroad engineer of the Cannonball, was known as the man who always brought the train in on time. He would blow the whistle, so it started off soft but would increase to a wail louder than a banshee before dying off so that people would recognize that whistle and know when Casey was driving past.

April 29, 1900, Casey brought the Cannonball into Memphis dead on time. As he was leaving, he found out one of the other engineers was sick and unable to make his run. So Casey volunteered to help out his friend. He pulled the train out of the station about eleven p.m., an hour and thirty-five minutes late. Casey was determined to make up the time. As soon as he could, he highballed out of Memphis (highballing means to go very fast and take a lot of risks to get where you are headed) and started making up for the lost time.

About four a.m., when he had nearly made up all the time on the run, Casey rounded a corner near Vaughn, Mississippi, and saw a stalled freight train on the track. He shouted for his fireman to jump. The fireman made it out alive, but Casey Jones died in the wreck, one hand on the brake and one on the whistle chord.

10. What type of story is Casey Jones?

Ⓐ fairy tale
Ⓑ fable
Ⓒ myth
Ⓓ folktale

End of Reading Literature

Chapter 2
Reading Informational Text

Test ID	8E014
Test Name	**Making Inferences Based on Textual Evidence**
Student Name	
Date	

1	Ⓐ Ⓑ Ⓒ Ⓓ	**6**	Ⓐ Ⓑ Ⓒ Ⓓ	**9**	Ⓐ Ⓑ Ⓒ Ⓓ
2	Ⓐ Ⓑ Ⓒ Ⓓ	**7 A**	Ⓐ Ⓑ Ⓒ Ⓓ	**10**	Ⓐ Ⓑ Ⓒ
3	Ⓐ Ⓑ Ⓒ Ⓓ	**7 B**	Ⓐ Ⓑ Ⓒ Ⓓ	**11**	Ⓐ Ⓑ Ⓒ Ⓓ
4	Ⓐ Ⓑ Ⓒ Ⓓ	**8 A**	Ⓐ Ⓑ Ⓒ Ⓓ	**12**	Ⓐ Ⓑ Ⓒ Ⓓ
5	Ⓐ Ⓑ Ⓒ Ⓓ	**8 B**	Ⓐ Ⓑ Ⓒ Ⓓ		

Lesson 1: Making Inferences Based on Textual Evidence

1. What is an inference?

- Ⓐ an answer that is clearly stated in the text
- Ⓑ a logical conclusion drawn from evidence in a text
- Ⓒ an opinion made from reading a text
- Ⓓ a direct quotation found in the text

2. What is the proper way to make a direct citation from a text?

- Ⓐ put the citation in italics
- Ⓑ underline the citation
- Ⓒ put the citation in quotes
- Ⓓ make the citation bold

3. What is/are the best way to cite evidence from a text?

- Ⓐ summarize
- Ⓑ paraphrase
- Ⓒ in quotes
- Ⓓ all of the above

Question 4-7 are based on the passage below

Stephen and Joseph Montgolfier were papermakers, but they had been interested in flying for many years. One night, in 1782, Joseph noticed something that gave him an idea. He was sitting in front of the fire when he saw some small pieces of scorched paper being carried up the chimney.

Soon afterwards, the brothers conducted an experiment. They lit a fire under a small silk bag, which was open at the bottom; at once, the bag rose to the ceiling. After this, Stephen and Joseph conducted many more experiments, both indoors and in the open air. Eventually, they built a huge balloon of linen and paper. On June 5th, 1783, they launched their balloon in the village of Annonay.

4. What evidence in the passage shows that the Montgolfier brothers discovered how to make a hot air balloon?

- Ⓐ "He was sitting in front of the fire when he saw some small pieces of scorched paper being carried up the chimney."
- Ⓑ "Eventually, they built a huge balloon of linen and paper. On June 5th, 1783, they launched their balloon in the village of Annonay."
- Ⓒ "After this, Stephen and Joseph conducted many more experiments, both indoors and in the open air."
- Ⓓ None of the above

5. What evidence in the text shows that the Montgolfier brothers launched the first successful hot air balloon?

Ⓐ "He was sitting in front of the fire when he saw some small pieces of scorched paper being carried up the chimney."

Ⓑ "Eventually, they built a huge balloon of linen and paper. On June 5th, 1783, they launched their balloon in the village of Annonay."

Ⓒ "After this, Stephen and Joseph conducted many more experiments, both indoors and in the open air."

Ⓓ None of the above

6. What evidence in the text could lead you to infer that the Montgolfier brothers' experienced some trial and error before successfully launching a hot air balloon?

Ⓐ "He was sitting in front of the fire when he saw some small pieces of scorched paper being carried up the chimney."

Ⓑ "Eventually, they built a huge balloon of linen and paper. On June 5th, 1783, they launched their balloon in the village of Annonay."

Ⓒ "After this, Stephen and Joseph conducted many more experiments, both indoors and in the open air."

Ⓓ None of the above

7. Part A
Which specific detail in the above passage describes the first experiment the brothers did?

Ⓐ Stephen and Joseph Montgolfier were papermakers, but they had been interested in flying for many years.

Ⓑ He was sitting in front of the fire when he saw some small pieces of scorched paper being carried up the chimney.

Ⓒ After this, Stephen and Joseph conducted many more experiments, both indoors and in the open air.

Ⓓ They lit a fire under a small silk bag, which was open at the bottom; at once, the bag rose to the ceiling.

Part B
The reader can tell from the article that Joseph Montgolfier was very observant because

Ⓐ He created a balloon from paper and linen.

Ⓑ He noticed the small pieces of burnt paper being carried up the chimney.

Ⓒ He found the best location to launch the balloon.

Ⓓ He was interested in flying.

TERRORISM— A CHALLENGE

Terrorism is one of the most serious threats and challenges that the world faces today. It is a war against democracy and a crime against humanity. It has crossed national boundaries and has international ramifications. Terrorism, in a way, is a new challenge to humanity in the 21st century.

Terrorism is violence used by a few unlawful, ruthless, heartless, and senseless criminals against fellow human beings. Terrorists have total disregard for human lives including their own. They commit crimes and cause bloodshed without any sense of guilt. To them, their cause is everything, and others are either for it or against it.

Violence is an essential part of terrorism. Terrorism is a systematic use of violence or the threat of violence to achieve specific goals. It attempts to use violence to cause widespread panic, fear, or terror to achieve its ultimate aim.

8. Part A
According to the above passage what is the most important aspect of terrorism?

- Ⓐ violence
- Ⓑ democracy
- Ⓒ national unity
- Ⓓ humanity

Part B
Which sentence explains who is targeted by terrorism?

- Ⓐ Terrorism is one of the most serious threats and challenges that the world faces today.
- Ⓑ It is a war against democracy and a crime against humanity.
- Ⓒ Terrorism is violence used by a few unlawful, ruthless, heartless, and senseless criminals against fellow human beings.
- Ⓓ both B and C

The Emperor Penguin is the only penguin species that breeds during the Antarctic winter. It treks 31–75 miles over the ice to breeding colonies, which may include thousands of penguins. The female lays a single egg, which is then incubated by the male while the female returns to the sea to feed; parents subsequently take turns foraging at sea and caring for their chick in the colony. The average lifespan of the Emperor Penguin is 20 years, although observations suggest that some Emperor Penguins may live to 50 years of age.

9. **What evidence in the text could lead you to infer both the male and female penguin share equally in the responsibility of raising the chick?**

Ⓐ "The average lifespan of the Emperor Penguin is 20 years,"
Ⓑ "The Emperor Penguin is the only penguin species that breeds during the Antarctic winter."
Ⓒ "…parents subsequently take turns foraging at sea and caring for their chick in the colony."
Ⓓ "…some Emperor Penguins may live to 50 years of age."

10. **What evidence in the text tells you what the penguins do to survive in the colony after the chick is born?**

Ⓐ "The average lifespan of the Emperor Penguin is 20 years,"
Ⓑ "The Emperor Penguin is the only penguin species that breeds during the Antarctic winter."
Ⓒ None of the above

Excerpt from the Foreword of **A Princess of Mars** by Edgar Rice Burroughs

My first recollection of Captain Carter is of the few months he spent at my father's home in Virginia, just prior to the opening of the Civil War. I was then a child of but five years, yet I well remember the tall, dark, smooth-faced, athletic man whom I called Uncle Jack.

He seemed always to be laughing; and he entered into the sports of the children with the same hearty good fellowship he displayed toward those pastimes in which the men and women of his own age indulged; or he would sit for an hour at a time entertaining my old grandmother with stories of his strange wild life in all parts of the world. We all loved him, and our slaves fairly worshipped the ground he trod.

He was a splendid specimen of manhood, standing a good two inches over six feet, broad of shoulder and narrow of hip, with the carriage of the trained fighting man. His features were regular and clear cut, his hair black and closely cropped, while his eyes were of a steel gray, reflecting a strong and loyal character, filled with fire and initiative. His manners were perfect, and his courtliness was that of a typical southern gentleman of the highest type.

11. **Based on the evidence in the text, what can you determine about Captain Carter's personality?**

    Ⓐ He was a happy man.
    Ⓑ He was a hard worker.
    Ⓒ He was ready to go to war.
    Ⓓ He was a friendly man.

12. **Based on the evidence in the text what historical event is about to happen?**

    Ⓐ World War II
    Ⓑ World War I
    Ⓒ Civil War
    Ⓓ The Revolutionary war

Test ID	8E015
Test Name	**Central Idea**
Student Name	
Date	

1	Ⓐ Ⓑ Ⓒ Ⓓ	6	Ⓐ Ⓑ Ⓒ Ⓓ	11 A	Ⓐ Ⓑ Ⓒ Ⓓ
2	Ⓐ Ⓑ Ⓒ Ⓓ	7	Ⓐ Ⓑ Ⓒ Ⓓ	11 B	Ⓐ Ⓑ Ⓒ Ⓓ
3	Ⓐ Ⓑ Ⓒ Ⓓ	8	Ⓐ Ⓑ Ⓒ Ⓓ	12	Ⓐ Ⓑ Ⓒ Ⓓ
4	Ⓐ Ⓑ Ⓒ Ⓓ	9	Ⓐ Ⓑ Ⓒ Ⓓ		
5	Ⓐ Ⓑ Ⓒ Ⓓ	10	Ⓐ Ⓑ Ⓒ Ⓓ		

Chapter 2 → Lesson 2: Central Idea

1. What is a central idea?

(A) the idea stated in the topic sentence
(B) the theme of a piece of literature
(C) a piece of informational text is mainly about someone
(D) the main idea of a piece of informational text

2. What statement(s) is/are true about a central idea?

(A) It can sometimes be found in the title of the text.
(B) It is supported by the details in the text.
(C) It covers the whole text.
(D) All of the above

3. When determining the central idea of a text, it is important not to confuse it with:

(A) the topic
(B) the details
(C) none of the above
(D) both A & B

Question 4 is based on the passage below

Stephen and Joseph Montgolfier were papermakers, but they had been interested in flying for many years. One night, in 1782, Joseph noticed something that gave him an idea. He was sitting in front of the fire when he saw some small pieces of scorched paper being carried up the chimney.

Soon afterwards, the brothers conducted an experiment. They lit a fire under a small silk bag, which was open at the bottom; at once, the bag rose to the ceiling. After this, Stephen and Joseph conducted many more experiments, both indoors and in the open air. Eventually, they built a huge balloon of linen and paper. On June 5th, 1783, they launched their balloon in the village of Annonay.

4. What is the central idea of this passage?

(A) The Montgolfier brothers were papermakers who became famous.
(B) The Montgolfier brothers theorized that hot air can be used to propel a balloon into the air.
(C) The Montgolfier brothers lost their jobs as papermakers because they were obsessed with their balloon.
(D) The Montgolfier brothers liked to experiment.

The Emperor Penguin is the only penguin species that breeds during the Antarctic winter. It treks 31–75 miles over the ice to breeding colonies, which may include thousands of penguins. The female lays a single egg, which is then incubated by the male while the female returns to the sea to feed; parents subsequently take turns foraging at sea and caring for their chick in the colony. The average lifespan of the Emperor Penguin is 20 years, although observations suggest that some Emperor Penguins may live to 50 years of age.

5. What is the central idea of this passage?

Ⓐ The movie, Happy Feet was inspired by Emperor Penguins.
Ⓑ The male Emperor Penguin sits on the egg while the mother hunts for food.
Ⓒ Female Emperor penguins lay their eggs in the Antarctic and both male and female take turns caring for the egg until it hatches.
Ⓓ Emperor Penguins live over 50 years.

Archaeology is the study of past human life and culture through systematically examining and interpreting the material remains left behind. These material remains include archaeological sites (e.g., settlements, building features, graves), as well as cultural materials or artifacts such as tools and pottery. Through the interpretation and classification of archaeological materials, archaeologists work to understand past human behavior. In some countries, archaeology is often historical or art historical, with a strong emphasis on culture history, archaeological sites, and artifacts such as art objects. In the New World, archaeology can be either a part of history and classical studies or anthropology.

The exact origins of archaeology as a discipline are uncertain. Excavations of ancient monuments and the collection of antiquities have been taking place for thousands of years. It was only in the 19th century, however, that the systematic study of the past through its physical remains underwent professionalization, which meant it began to be carried out in a manner recognizable to modern students of archaeology.

6. What is the central idea of this passage?

Ⓐ the study of the origin of archaeology
Ⓑ the study of archaeology
Ⓒ the study of modern archaeology and anthropology
Ⓓ the study of the human past

7. What does the passage suggest about archaeologists?

Ⓐ They study past human life and culture by examining materials left by early humans.
Ⓑ They study humans and their interaction with their surroundings.
Ⓒ They study humans and their families by looking at the things they left behind.
Ⓓ They study art history.

Question 8 is based on the passage below

Quinoa is a grain like seed. It is considered a whole grain and is cooked in much the same way as rice. Quinoa has many health benefits including nine essential amino acids and is cholesterol free. Additionally quinoa is gluten-free and kosher. Quinoa is a good source of protein and easily digestible.

8. What is the central idea of the passage above?

Ⓐ the health benefits of quinoa
Ⓑ how to cook quinoa
Ⓒ why people should eat quinoa
Ⓓ why people should cook quinoa

Question 9 is based on the passage below

Cooking quinoa is much like cooking rice. Depending on the sort of quinoa you purchase, you may have to rinse the seed-like spores before cooking. Be sure to check the label. Boil two cups of water, vegetable stock, chicken broth or other liquid of your choice. Add one cup of raw (rinsed if necessary) quinoa and simmer for about twenty minutes. It doesn't take long for quinoa to cook up moist and tender.

9. What is the central idea of this passage?

Ⓐ the health benefits of quinoa
Ⓑ how to cook quinoa
Ⓒ quinoa as a meat replacement
Ⓓ none of the above

Question 10 is based on the passage below

University of California Berkeley scientists confirmed that a cluster of fossilized bones found in Silicon Valley are likely the remains of a mammoth. The giant beast would have roamed the area between 10,000 and 40,000 years ago. A pair of elephant-like tusks, a huge pelvic bone and the animal's rib cage were found by an amateur naturalist who was walking a dog along a canal near San Jose's Guadalupe River. It could be the remains of a Columbian mammoth, according to paleontologists who expect to study the site.

10. What is the central idea of the above passage?

Ⓐ Mammoth fossils have been found in the Silicone Valley.
Ⓑ Fossils are in California.
Ⓒ Mammoths roamed North America.
Ⓓ Mammoths are roaming the Silicone Valley in California.

Question 11 is based on the passage below

Marathon

Training for a marathon takes hard work and perseverance. It is not something you can do on the spur of the moment. Preparing for a marathon takes months, particularly if you have never run a marathon before. The official distance of a full marathon is 26.2 miles. In 2005, the average time to complete a marathon in the United States was 4 hours 32 minutes 8 seconds for men and 5 hours 6 minutes 8 seconds for women.

Most people who run marathons are not trying to win. Many runners try to beat their own best time. Some compare their time to other runners in the same gender and age group. Some people set time-oriented goals, such as finishing under four hours, while others try to complete the race without slowing to a walk. Many beginners simply hope to finish the marathon.

Trainers recommend that beginners maintain a consistent running schedule for six weeks prior to even starting a marathon training program. The purpose of this is to allow the body to adapt to the various physical demands of long-distance running. First-time marathon runners should train by running four days a week for at least four months, increasing distance by no more than ten percent weekly. As race day approaches, runners should taper their runs, reducing the strain on their bodies and resting before the marathon. It is important not to overexert yourself during training because that can lead to a lot of injuries. Most common injuries are spraining of the knees and ankles. These sprains can hinder the training.

Before the race, it is important to stretch in order to keep muscles limber. Staying hydrated is also important, but there is a danger in drinking too much water. If a runner drinks too much water, they may experience a dangerous condition called hyponatremia, a drop of sodium levels in the blood. So only drink water when you are thirsty. During the race, trainers recommend maintaining a steady pace. It is normal to feel sore after a marathon. Light exercise will help sore muscles heal faster.

Some people run marathons in pairs or groups. Training for and running a marathon with another person or group of people can make the experience more enjoyable and more rewarding. A running partner might be just the motivation you need to show up for an early morning run instead of rolling over to hit the snooze button. And, when you cross the finish line together, you can share the satisfaction of reaching your common goal.

Usually thousands of people sign up and run a marathon. Most people finish the race. The thrill of running a marathon for the first time is unbelievable. The training sessions are harder if you have never run before. But it is unbelievable what ones' body can do when one puts his/her mind to it. Having a good coach to support you makes all the difference in training for a marathon.

The daily runs are very important. Strength training and core training are also very important. The health benefits you gain from training are tremendous. Your core muscles grow stronger, and you will have tighter thighs and gluts. Your heart will be much stronger, and you can maintain lower cholesterol and blood sugar levels. Overall, you will look better and become healthier.

Nothing can explain how people feel when they reach that finish line at the end of the race. All the hard work and months of training feel worthwhile. The feeling of accomplishing something great overtakes you. It is great to run a marathon, but it is even greater to finish it.

11. Part A
How would you go about determining the central idea of this passage?

Ⓐ read the title
Ⓑ read the passage
Ⓒ pay attention to the details
Ⓓ all of the above

Part B
What is the central idea of the passage?

Ⓐ the health benefits of running of a marathon
Ⓑ how to run a marathon
Ⓒ what it takes to prepare for and run a marathon
Ⓓ none of the above

Learning how to ride a bike is no easy task. Most people learn as children and mount their first bicycle with training wheels mounted on the sides of the back tires. Those training wheels eventually come off. When that happens, usually someone runs behind the bicycle, holding the back of the seat as the rider learns to balance on two wheels. As the runner runs back and forth down the street, the rider eventually picks up on how to lean to stay up on two wheels. Eventually, the runner lets go of the seat, and the rider rides off on his or her own.

12. What is the central idea of this passage?

Ⓐ Learning how to run behind a new rider.
Ⓑ How to take training wheels off a bicycle.
Ⓒ Learning how to ride a two wheel bicycle.
Ⓓ None of the above

Test ID	8E016
Test Name	**Connections and Distinctions**
Student Name	
Date	

1	Ⓐ Ⓑ Ⓒ Ⓓ	6 A	Ⓐ Ⓑ Ⓒ Ⓓ
2	Ⓐ Ⓑ Ⓒ Ⓓ	6 B	Ⓐ Ⓑ Ⓒ Ⓓ
3	Ⓐ Ⓑ Ⓒ Ⓓ	7	Ⓐ Ⓑ Ⓒ Ⓓ
4	Ⓐ Ⓑ Ⓒ Ⓓ	8	Ⓐ Ⓑ Ⓒ Ⓓ
5	Ⓐ Ⓑ Ⓒ Ⓓ	9	Ⓐ Ⓑ Ⓒ Ⓓ

Date of Completion:_____   Score:_____
Chapter 2 → Lesson 3: Connections and Distinctions

1. What does it mean to make a distinction?

- Ⓐ to find a similarity
- Ⓑ to find a difference
- Ⓒ to draw a conclusion
- Ⓓ to point out a fact

2. What does it mean to make a connection?

- Ⓐ to find a similarity
- Ⓑ to find a difference
- Ⓒ to draw a conclusion
- Ⓓ to point out a fact

Question 3 and 4 are based on the passage below

Archaeology is the study of past human life and culture through systematically examining and interpreting the material remains left behind. These material remains include archaeological sites (e.g., settlements, building features, graves), as well as cultural materials or artifacts such as tools and pottery. Through the interpretation and classification of archaeological materials, archaeologists work to understand past human behavior. In some countries, archaeology is often historical or art historical, with a strong emphasis on culture history, archaeological sites, and artifacts such as art objects. In the New World, archaeology can be either a part of history and classical studies or anthropology.

The exact origins of archaeology as a discipline are uncertain. Excavations of ancient monuments and the collection of antiquities have been taking place for thousands of years. It was only in the 19th century, however, that the systematic study of the past through its physical remains underwent professionalization, which meant it began to be carried out in a manner recognizable to modern students of archaeology.

3. What is similar between New World archaeology and archaeology of the past?

- Ⓐ They both focus on history.
- Ⓑ They both focus on art.
- Ⓒ They both focus on culture.
- Ⓓ all of the above

LumosLearning.com   111

4. **Based on the information in the article, where would a good place to examine archaeology be?**

    Ⓐ online
    Ⓑ at a museum
    Ⓒ in a book
    Ⓓ all of the above

Question 5 is based on the passage below

Cooking quinoa is much like cooking rice. Depending on the sort of quinoa you purchase, you may have to rinse the seed-like spores before cooking. Be sure to check the label. Boil two cups of water, vegetable stock, chicken broth or other liquid of your choice. Add one cup of raw (rinsed if necessary) quinoa and simmer for about twenty minutes. It doesn't take long for quinoa to cook up moist and tender.

5. **What is one distinction that the passage reminds you to take?**

    Ⓐ The type of quinoa you buy will determine if you have to rinse.
    Ⓑ There are different types of quinoa that taste differently.
    Ⓒ Always feel the quinoa before buying it.
    Ⓓ The type of liquid to use is your choice.

Question 6 is based on the passage below

Marathon

Training for a marathon takes hard work and perseverance. It is not something you can do on the spur of the moment. Preparing for a marathon takes months, particularly if you have never run a marathon before. The official distance of a full marathon is 26.2 miles. In 2005, the average time to complete a marathon in the United States was 4 hours 32 minutes 8 seconds for men and 5 hours 6 minutes 8 seconds for women.

Most people who run marathons are not trying to win. Many runners try to beat their own best time. Some compare their time to other runners in the same gender and age group. Some people set time-oriented goals, such as finishing under four hours, while others try to complete the race without slowing to a walk. Many beginners simply hope to finish the marathon.

Trainers recommend that beginners maintain a consistent running schedule for six weeks prior to even starting a marathon training program. The purpose of this is to allow the body to adapt to the various physical demands of long-distance running. First-time marathon runners should train by running four days a week for at least four months, increasing distance by no more than ten percent weekly. As race day approaches, runners should taper their runs, reducing the strain on their bodies and resting before the marathon. It is important not to overexert yourself during training because that can lead to a lot of injuries. Most common injuries are spraining of the knees and ankles. These sprains can hinder the training.

Before the race, it is important to stretch in order to keep muscles limber. Staying hydrated is also important, but there is a danger in drinking too much water. If a runner drinks too much water, they may experience a dangerous condition called hyponatremia, a drop of sodium levels in the blood. So only drink water when you are thirsty. During the race, trainers recommend maintaining a steady pace. It is normal to feel sore after a marathon. Light exercise will help sore muscles heal faster.

Some people run marathons in pairs or groups. Training for and running a marathon with another person or group of people can make the experience more enjoyable and more rewarding. A running partner might be just the motivation you need to show up for an early morning run instead of rolling over to hit the snooze button. And, when you cross the finish line together, you can share the satisfaction of reaching your common goal.

Usually, thousands of people sign up and run a marathon. Most people finish the race. The thrill of running a marathon for the first time is unbelievable. The training sessions are harder if you have never run before. But it is unbelievable what ones' body can do when one puts their mind to it. Having a good coach to support you makes all the difference in training for a marathon.

The daily runs are very important. Strength training and core training are also very important.

The health benefits you gain from training are tremendous. Your core muscles grow stronger, and you will have tighter thighs and gluts. Your heart will be much stronger, and you can maintain lower cholesterol and blood sugar levels. Overall, you will look better and become healthier.

Nothing can explain how people feel when they reach that finish line at the end of the race. All the hard work and months of training feel worthwhile. The feeling of accomplishing something great overtakes you. It is great to run a marathon, but it is even greater to finish it.

6. **Part A**
   How is a marathon competition different than most competitions?

   Ⓐ Runners compete against themselves to beat past times.
   Ⓑ Runners do not compete against each other.
   Ⓒ Runners set their own personal records.
   Ⓓ All of the above

Part B
What makes marathon running similar to other competitive sports?

Ⓐ health benefits
Ⓑ trophies
Ⓒ winning
Ⓓ numbers of people

Question 7 is based on the passage below

You read a research study that says eating a candy bar made of dark chocolate every day is good for your heart in the long run. The study followed the health of a large group of people over the course of ten years. You notice in fine print at the end of the research that the study was conducted by a major chocolate company.

7. What connection can you make with this study and other commercials you see on TV?

Ⓐ The study must be true if it is published.
Ⓑ Advertising agencies sometimes minimize major facts to help sell products.
Ⓒ Studies in all commercials are conducted by one research company.
Ⓓ Dark chocolate is good for your heart.

Question 8 and 9 are based on the passage below

From Chapter 1 of **Bullets and Billets** by Bruce Bainsfather

I stood in a queue of Gordons, Seaforths, Worcesters, etc., slowly moving up one, until, finally arriving at the companion (nearly said staircase), I tobogganed down into the hold, and spent what was left of the night dealing out those rations. Having finished, at last, I came to the surface again, and now, as the transport glided along through the dirty waters of the river, and as I gazed at the motley collection of Frenchmen on the various wharves, and saw a variety of soldiery, and a host of other warlike "props," I felt acutely that now I was in the war at last—the real thing! For some time, I had been rehearsing in England; but that was over now, and here I was—in the common or garden vernacular—"in the soup."

8. Based on the context of the phrase "in the soup," what can you conclude the author is saying?

Ⓐ He's happy he has reached his destination.
Ⓑ He's hungry and ready to eat.
Ⓒ He is entering a bad situation.
Ⓓ He came to the surface and spent time.

9. What conclusion can you draw about this passage?

Ⓐ The narrator is heading into war.
Ⓑ The narrator is going on a trip.
Ⓒ The narrator is frustrated about his journey.
Ⓓ The narrator likes rivers.

Test ID	8E017
Test Name	**Determining Meaning of Words**
Student Name	
Date	

1	Ⓐ Ⓑ Ⓒ Ⓓ	6 A	Ⓐ Ⓑ Ⓒ Ⓓ	
2	Ⓐ Ⓑ Ⓒ Ⓓ	6 B	Ⓐ Ⓑ Ⓒ Ⓓ	
3	Ⓐ Ⓑ Ⓒ Ⓓ	7	Ⓐ Ⓑ Ⓒ Ⓓ	
4	Ⓐ Ⓑ Ⓒ Ⓓ	8 A	Ⓐ Ⓑ Ⓒ Ⓓ	
5	Ⓐ Ⓑ Ⓒ Ⓓ	8 B	Ⓐ Ⓑ Ⓒ Ⓓ	

Chapter 2 → Lesson 4: Determining Meaning of Words

1. What is connotation?

- (A) A dictionary definition
- (B) What a word means based on its context in a story
- (C) A word with multiple meanings
- (D) An opinion based on fact

2. What is denotation?

- (A) A dictionary definition
- (B) What a word means based on its context in a story
- (C) A word that has a meaning that has changed over time
- (D) An opinion based on fact

Question 3 is based on the passage below

The Emperor Penguin is the only penguin species that breeds during the Antarctic winter. It treks 31–75 miles over the ice to breeding colonies, which may include thousands of penguins. The female lays a single egg, which is then incubated by the male while the female returns to the sea to feed; parents subsequently take turns foraging at sea and caring for their chick in the colony. The average lifespan of the Emperor Penguin is 20 years, although observations suggest that some Emperor Penguins may live to 50 years of age.

3. Based on how the word "trek" is used in the passage, determine its meaning.

- (A) to fly a long-distance
- (B) to circulate in a specific area
- (C) to walk a long-distance
- (D) to live a long life

Question 4 and 5 are based on the passage below

Archaeology is the study of past human life and culture through <u>systematically</u> examining and interpreting the material remains left behind. These material remains include archaeological sites (e.g., settlements, building features, graves), as well as cultural materials or artifacts such as tools and pottery. Through the interpretation and classification of archaeological materials, archaeologists work to understand past human behavior. In some countries, archaeology is often historical or art historical, with a strong emphasis on culture history, archaeological sites, and artifacts such as art objects. In the New World, archaeology can be either a part of history and classical studies or anthropology.

The exact origins of archaeology as a discipline are uncertain. Excavations of ancient monuments and the collection of antiquities have been taking place for thousands of years. It was only in the

19th century, however, that the systematic study of the past through its physical remains underwent <u>professionalization</u>, which meant it began to be carried out in a manner recognizable to modern students of archaeology.

4. What does the underlined word "professionalization" mean?

Ⓐ the way a field of study turns into a professional job
Ⓑ the way an artifact turns into a noted antique
Ⓒ the way a civilization is recovered and displayed
Ⓓ to study art history

5. What does it mean to do something "systematically"?

Ⓐ to follow very specific instructions
Ⓑ to use the scientific method of trial and error
Ⓒ to record the process you followed to do something
Ⓓ none of the above

> **Question 6 and 7 are based on the passage below**

Marathon

Training for a marathon takes hard work and perseverance. It is not something you can do on the spur of the moment. Preparing for a marathon takes months, particularly if you have never run a marathon before. The official distance of a full marathon is 26.2 miles. In 2005, the average time to complete a marathon in the United States was 4 hours 32 minutes 8 seconds for men and 5 hours 6 minutes 8 seconds for women.

Most people who run marathons are not trying to win. Many runners try to beat their own best time. Some compare their time to other runners in the same gender and age group. Some people set time-oriented goals, such as finishing under four hours, while others try to complete the race without slowing to a walk. Many beginners simply hope to finish the marathon.

Trainers recommend that beginners maintain a consistent running schedule for six weeks prior to even starting a marathon training program. The purpose of this is to allow the body to adapt to the various physical demands of long-distance running. First-time marathon runners should train by running four days a week for at least four months, increasing distance by no more than ten percent weekly. As race day approaches, runners should taper their runs, reducing the strain on their bodies and resting before the marathon. It is important not to overexert yourself during training because that can lead to a lot of injuries. Most common injuries are spraining of the knees and ankles. These sprains can hinder the training.

Before the race, it is important to stretch in order to keep muscles limber. Staying hydrated is also important, but there is a danger in drinking too much water. If a runner drinks too much water, they may experience a dangerous condition called hyponatremia, a drop of sodium levels in the blood. So only drink water when you are thirsty. During the race, trainers recommend maintaining a steady pace. It is normal to feel sore after a marathon. Light exercise will help sore muscles heal faster.

Some people run marathons in pairs or groups. Training for and running a marathon with another person or group of people can make the experience more enjoyable and more rewarding. A running partner might be just the motivation you need to show up for an early morning run instead of rolling over to hit the snooze button. And, when you cross the finish line together, you can share the satisfaction of reaching your common goal.

Usually, thousands of people sign up and run a marathon. Most people finish the race. The thrill of running a marathon for the first time is unbelievable. The training sessions are harder if you have never run before. But it is unbelievable what ones' body can do when one puts their mind to it. Having a good coach to support you makes all the difference in training for a marathon.

The daily runs are very important. Strength training and core training are also very important.

The health benefits you gain from training are tremendous. Your core muscles grow stronger, and you will have tighter thighs and gluts. Your heart will be much stronger, and you can maintain lower cholesterol and blood sugar levels. Overall, you will look better and become healthier.

Nothing can explain how people feel when they reach that finish line at the end of the race. All the hard work and months of training feel worthwhile. The feeling of accomplishing something great overtakes you. It is great to run a marathon, but it is even greater to finish it.

6. Part A
What does the phrase "overexert" (third paragraph) mean?

Ⓐ go over the amount of time you need to run
Ⓑ go over the distance you need to run
Ⓒ do more than your body can handle
Ⓓ drink too much water

Part B
What does the phrase "spur of the moment" (first paragraph) mean?

Ⓐ in the moment, without thinking
Ⓑ at the last minute
Ⓒ on a horse wearing spurs
Ⓓ taking time to train

7. How does the phrase "spur of the moment" add to the tone of the passage?

Ⓐ   It creates a humorous tone so the readers laugh and enjoy the piece.
Ⓑ   It creates a serious tone necessary to show how hard running a marathon is.
Ⓒ   It creates a factual tone so readers can study before training.
Ⓓ   It creates a reminder of how important training is.

Question 8 is based on the passage below

From Chapter 1 of **Bullets and Billets** by Bruce Bainsfather

I stood in a queue of Gordons, Seaforths, Worcesters, etc., slowly moving up one, until, finally arriving at the companion (nearly said staircase), I tobogganed down into the hold, and spent what was left of the night dealing out those rations. Having finished, at last, I came to the surface again, and now, as the transport glided along through the dirty waters of the river, and as I gazed at the motley collection of Frenchmen on the various wharves, and saw a variety of soldiery, and a host of other warlike "props," I felt acutely that now I was in the war at last—the real thing! For some time, I had been rehearsing in England; but that was over now, and here I was—in the common or garden vernacular—"in the soup."

8. Part A
Based on how they are used to begin the passage, what are "Gordons, Seaforths, and Worcesters?

Ⓐ   Ranks in an army
Ⓑ   Types of holding facilities on a ship
Ⓒ   Different destinations on the journey
Ⓓ   None of the above

Part B
The author is using what type of figurative language to compare war to a theater in the above passage.

Ⓐ   implied metaphor
Ⓑ   simile
Ⓒ   imagery
Ⓓ   allusion

Test ID	8E018
Test Name	**Analyzing Structures in Text**
Student Name	
Date	

1	Ⓐ Ⓑ Ⓒ Ⓓ	6	Ⓐ Ⓑ Ⓒ Ⓓ	11 A	Ⓐ Ⓑ Ⓒ Ⓓ
2	Ⓐ Ⓑ Ⓒ Ⓓ	7	Ⓐ Ⓑ Ⓒ Ⓓ	11 B	Ⓐ Ⓑ Ⓒ Ⓓ
3	Ⓐ Ⓑ Ⓒ Ⓓ	8	Ⓐ Ⓑ Ⓒ Ⓓ	11 C	Ⓐ Ⓑ Ⓒ Ⓓ
4	Ⓐ Ⓑ Ⓒ Ⓓ	9	Ⓐ Ⓑ Ⓒ Ⓓ	12 A	Ⓐ Ⓑ Ⓒ Ⓓ
5	Ⓐ Ⓑ Ⓒ Ⓓ	10	Ⓐ Ⓑ Ⓒ Ⓓ	12 B	Ⓐ Ⓑ Ⓒ Ⓓ

Chapter 2 → Lesson 5: Analyzing Structures in Text

1. What should you look at when analyzing the structure of a piece of text?

Ⓐ the genre of writing
Ⓑ the author's purpose
Ⓒ the types of transition words that are being used
Ⓓ all of the above

2. What type of writing has the following literary elements: characters, conflict, setting, and plot?

Ⓐ nonfiction
Ⓑ fiction
Ⓒ technical
Ⓓ poetry

3. If you saw words such as, "unlike", "as well as", "on the other hand", and "in contrast", what would you think the author's purpose was?

Ⓐ to persuade
Ⓑ to compare
Ⓒ to entertain
Ⓓ wouldn't be able to tell

Question 4 and 5 are based on the passage below

Stephen and Joseph Montgolfier were papermakers, but they had been interested in flying for many years. One night, in 1782, Joseph noticed something that gave him an idea. He was sitting in front of the fire when he saw some small pieces of scorched paper being carried up the chimney.

Soon afterwards, the brothers conducted an experiment. They lit a fire under a small silk bag, which was open at the bottom; at once, the bag rose to the ceiling. After this, Stephen and Joseph conducted many more experiments, both indoors and in the open air. Eventually, they built a huge balloon of linen and paper. On June 5th, 1783, they launched their balloon in the village of Annonay.

4. What would change this passage into an essay?

Ⓐ Adding an introductory paragraph and a conclusion.
Ⓑ Adding more details to the experiments.
Ⓒ Adding nothing, it is already an essay.
Ⓓ Rewriting it as a personal narrative.

5. What type of text structure is used in this passage?

    (A) sequence
    (B) compare/contrast
    (C) cause/effect
    (D) description

Question 6 is based on the passage below

The Emperor Penguin is the only penguin species that breeds during the Antarctic winter. It treks 31–75 miles over the ice to breeding colonies, which may include thousands of penguins. The female lays a single egg, which is then incubated by the male while the female returns to the sea to feed; parents subsequently take turns foraging at sea and caring for their chick in the colony. The average lifespan of the Emperor Penguin is 20 years, although observations suggest that some Emperor Penguins may live to 50 years of age.

6. What type of text structure is used in the passage above?

    (A) sequence
    (B) compare/contrast
    (C) description
    (D) cause/effect

Question 7 is based on the passage below

Archaeology is the study of past human life and culture through systematically examining and interpreting the material remains left behind. These material remains include archaeological sites (e.g., settlements, building features, graves), as well as cultural materials or artifacts such as tools and pottery. Through the interpretation and classification of archaeological materials, archaeologists work to understand past human behavior. In some countries, archaeology is often historical or art historical, with a strong emphasis on culture history, archaeological sites, and artifacts such as art objects. In the New World, archaeology can be either a part of history and classical studies or anthropology.

The exact origins of archaeology as a discipline are uncertain. Excavations of ancient monuments and the collection of antiquities have been taking place for thousands of years. It was only in the 19th century, however, that the systematic study of the past through its physical remains underwent professionalization, which meant it began to be carried out in a manner recognizable to modern students of archaeology.

"Archaeology is the study of past human life and culture through systematically examining and interpreting the material remains left behind."

7. The author uses this as the opening line to his article in order to:

Ⓐ give the reader a base to build their understanding of archaeology
Ⓑ tell why archaeology is important
Ⓒ give the reader an idea of what the article is going to be about
Ⓓ both A and C

Question 8 is based on the sentence below

"Through the interpretation and classification of archaeological materials, archaeologists work to understand past human behavior."

8. Why is this sentence included?

Ⓐ to give an example of why archaeology is important
Ⓑ to show the technical side of archaeology
Ⓒ to show the process of archaeology
Ⓓ to show how archaeology has changed

Question 9 is based on the sentence below

"Excavations of ancient monuments and the collection of antiquities have been taking place for thousands of years."

9. Why was this sentence included?

Ⓐ to clarify what archaeology is
Ⓑ to show that archaeology is not something that was supported long ago
Ⓒ to show that archaeology is a fairly modern concept
Ⓓ to explain that some form of archaeology has been happening for a very long time

Question 10 is based on the passage below

Marathon

Training for a marathon takes hard work and perseverance. It is not something you can do on the spur of the moment. Preparing for a marathon takes months, particularly if you have never run a marathon before. The official distance of a full marathon is 26.2 miles. In 2005, the average time to complete a marathon in the United States was 4 hours 32 minutes 8 seconds for men and 5 hours 6 minutes 8 seconds for women.

Most people who run marathons are not trying to win. Many runners try to beat their own best time. Some compare their time to other runners in the same gender and age group. Some people set time-oriented goals, such as finishing under four hours, while others try to complete the race without slowing to a walk. Many beginners simply hope to finish the marathon.

Trainers recommend that beginners maintain a consistent running schedule for six weeks prior to even starting a marathon training program. The purpose of this is to allow the body to adapt to the various physical demands of long-distance running. First-time marathon runners should train by running four days a week for at least four months, increasing distance by no more than ten percent weekly. As race day approaches, runners should taper their runs, reducing the strain on their bodies and resting before the marathon. It is important not to overexert yourself during training because that can lead to a lot of injuries. Most common injuries are spraining of the knees and ankles. These sprains can hinder the training.

Before the race, it is important to stretch in order to keep muscles limber. Staying hydrated is also important, but there is a danger in drinking too much water. If a runner drinks too much water, they may experience a dangerous condition called hyponatremia, a drop of sodium levels in the blood. So only drink water when you are thirsty. During the race, trainers recommend maintaining a steady pace. It is normal to feel sore after a marathon. Light exercise will help sore muscles heal faster.

Some people run marathons in pairs or groups. Training for and running a marathon with another person or group of people can make the experience more enjoyable and more rewarding. A running partner might be just the motivation you need to show up for an early morning run instead of rolling over to hit the snooze button. And, when you cross the finish line together, you can share the satisfaction of reaching your common goal.

Usually, thousands of people sign up and run a marathon. Most people finish the race. The thrill of running a marathon for the first time is unbelievable. The training sessions are harder if you have never run before. But it is unbelievable what ones' body can do when one puts their mind to it. Having a good coach to support you makes all the difference in training for a marathon.

The daily runs are very important. Strength training and core training are also very important.

The health benefits you gain from training are tremendous. Your core muscles grow stronger, and you will have tighter thighs and gluts. Your heart will be much stronger, and you can maintain lower cholesterol and blood sugar levels. Overall, you will look better and become healthier.

Nothing can explain how people feel when they reach that finish line at the end of the race. All the hard work and months of training feel worthwhile. The feeling of accomplishing something great overtakes you. It is great to run a marathon, but it is even greater to finish it.

"Nothing can explain how people feel when they reach that finish line at the end of the race. All the hard work and months of training feel worthwhile."

10. Why are these two sentences included in the conclusion?

Ⓐ leave the reader with a positive reason to run a marathon
Ⓑ persuade the reader that anyone can run a marathon
Ⓒ show the reader that running a marathon is not difficult
Ⓓ change the tone of the article

Question 11 is based on the passages below

The Eagle	First Flight
Far from the habitations of humans and their petty quarrels, there once lived on top of a rugged hill, an old eagle. When the fragrant morning breeze blew through his nest, the eagle would shake his feathers and spread out his wings. When the sun rose high and the world below engaged itself in its unceasing fight for survival, the eagle would take off from the hill-top and circle majestically over the valley and its dwellers, the fields and the running brooks. If he saw something worthwhile, such as a hare or a rat, a pigeon or a chick, he would swoop down on it like lightning, fetch it to his nest, and devour it. He would then inspect the surroundings once again.	The young seagull was alone on his ledge. His two brothers and his sister had already flown away the day before. He had afraid to fly with them. Somehow, when he had taken a little run forward to the brink of the ledge and attempted to flap his wings he became afraid. The great expanse of sea stretched down beneath, and it was such a long way down - miles down. He felt certain that his wings would never support him; so he bent his head and ran away, back to the little hole under the ledge where he slept at night. Even when each of his brothers and his little sister, whose wings were far shorter than his own, ran to the brink, flapped their wings, and flew away, he failed to muster up courage to take that plunge, which appeared to him so desperate. His father and mother had come around calling to him shrilly, upbraiding him, and threatening to let him starve on his ledge unless he flew away; but for the life of him he could not move.

11. Part A
After reading the two passages, what contrast can be made?

Ⓐ Passage one is about an eagle and passage two is about a seagull.
Ⓑ The eagle is old and the seagull is young.
Ⓒ The old eagle has mastered flying where as the young seagull is afraid of flying.
Ⓓ all of the above

Part B
While the eagle is a confident flyer, the seagull is _____.

Ⓐ afraid to fly.
Ⓑ also a confident flyer.
Ⓒ a smaller bird.
Ⓓ excited to fly.

Part C
The process of learning how to fly is discussed in _____.

Ⓐ both passages.
Ⓑ neither passage.
Ⓒ "The Eagle"
Ⓓ "First Flight"

Question 12 is based on the passages below

Archaeology	History of Mankind
Archaeology is the study of past human life and culture through systematically examining and interpreting the material remains left behind. These material remains include archaeological sites (e.g., settlements, building features, graves), as well as cultural materials or artifacts such as tools and pottery. Through the interpretation and classification of archaeological materials, archaeologists work to understand past human behavior. In some countries, archaeology is often historical or art historical, with a strong emphasis on cultural history, archaeological sites, and artifacts such as art objects. In the New World, archaeology can be either a part of history and classical studies or anthropology. The exact origins of archaeology as a discipline are uncertain. Excavations of ancient monuments and the collection of antiquities have been taking place for thousands of years. It was only in the 19th century, however, that the systematic study of the past through its physical remains began to be carried out in a manner recognizable to modern students of archaeology.	History is about events that happened in the past. It is like an interesting and exciting series of stories. However, these stories are not like the many fairy tales you may have read. These stories are about real people and events that have really happened. It tells us about the lives of great men. Some were great rulers who fought battles and conquered lands. Some were famous teachers, writers, explorers, scientists, artists, and musicians. They performed great deeds and showed people how to lead productive lives. History tells us how early civilization began. It describes how those people lived, how they got their food, and how they built their villages and cities. How do we have a record of events from long ago? In recent years. People have excavated ruins of old cities that were buried deep beneath the ground. We can learn about the people who lived in the lost cities by carefully examining artifacts found in these sites. Some of the items include sharp stones used for hunting, pots, and pans used for cooking and beads and necklaces used as jewelry. These items offer some clues about the life of people who lived during that time.

12. Part A
Both passages focus on _____.

Ⓐ the method of finding artifacts.
Ⓑ learning more about the past.
Ⓒ why history is taught in school.
Ⓓ events in history.

Part B
What comparison can be made between the two passages?

Ⓐ Both passages are about human life in the past.
Ⓑ Both passages are about mummies.
Ⓒ Both A and B.
Ⓓ None of the above.

Test ID	8E019
Test Name	**Author's Point of View**
Student Name	
Date	

1	Ⓐ Ⓑ Ⓒ Ⓓ	6	Ⓐ Ⓑ Ⓒ Ⓓ	11	Ⓐ Ⓑ Ⓒ Ⓓ
2	Ⓐ Ⓑ Ⓒ Ⓓ	7	Ⓐ Ⓑ Ⓒ Ⓓ		
3	Ⓐ Ⓑ Ⓒ Ⓓ	8	Ⓐ Ⓑ Ⓒ Ⓓ		
4	Ⓐ Ⓑ Ⓒ Ⓓ	9	Ⓐ Ⓑ Ⓒ Ⓓ		
5	Ⓐ Ⓑ Ⓒ Ⓓ	10	Ⓐ Ⓑ Ⓒ Ⓓ		

Chapter 2 → Lesson 6: Author's Point of View

1. What is point of view?

- Ⓐ   a character's view of the action in a story
- Ⓑ   the perspective from which a story is told
- Ⓒ   where the author is when writing a story
- Ⓓ   the view of the character in the story

2. Which type of point of view uses the pronouns "I, me, and my"?

- Ⓐ   first person
- Ⓑ   third person omniscient
- Ⓒ   third person limited
- Ⓓ   second person

3. When the narrator is one of the characters in the story, what point of view is the story being told from?

- Ⓐ   First person
- Ⓑ   Third person omniscient
- Ⓒ   Third person limited
- Ⓓ   second person

4. Which of the following is true of the point of view known as third person omniscient?

- Ⓐ   The narrator is not a character in the story.
- Ⓑ   The narrator is a character in the story.
- Ⓒ   The narrator only knows that which he or she sees and hears.
- Ⓓ   The narrator is talking about himself

5. Which of the following is true of the point of view known as third person limited?

- Ⓐ   The narrator is not a character in the story.
- Ⓑ   The narrator is a character in the story.
- Ⓒ   The narrator only knows that which he or she sees and hears.
- Ⓓ   The narrator knows everything about all of the characters.

6. Which type of narrator is the most reliable?

- Ⓐ   first person
- Ⓑ   third person limited
- Ⓒ   third person omniscient
- Ⓓ   second person

Marathon

Training for a marathon takes hard work and perseverance. It is not something you can do on the spur of the moment. Preparing for a marathon takes months, particularly if you have never run a marathon before. The official distance of a full marathon is 26.2 miles. In 2005, the average time to complete a marathon in the United States was 4 hours 32 minutes 8 seconds for men and 5 hours 6 minutes 8 seconds for women.

Most people who run marathons are not trying to win. Many runners try to beat their own best time. Some compare their time to other runners in the same gender and age group. Some people set time-oriented goals, such as finishing under four hours, while others try to complete the race without slowing to a walk. Many beginners simply hope to finish the marathon.

Trainers recommend that beginners maintain a consistent running schedule for six weeks prior to even starting a marathon training program. The purpose of this is to allow the body to adapt to the various physical demands of long-distance running. First-time marathon runners should train by running four days a week for at least four months, increasing distance by no more than ten percent weekly. As race day approaches, runners should taper their runs, reducing the strain on their bodies and resting before the marathon. It is important not to overexert yourself during training because that can lead to a lot of injuries. Most common injuries are spraining of the knees and ankles. These sprains can hinder the training.

Before the race, it is important to stretch in order to keep muscles limber. Staying hydrated is also important, but there is a danger in drinking too much water. If a runner drinks too much water, they may experience a dangerous condition called hyponatremia, a drop of sodium levels in the blood. So only drink water when you are thirsty. During the race, trainers recommend maintaining a steady pace. It is normal to feel sore after a marathon. Light exercise will help sore muscles heal faster.

Some people run marathons in pairs or groups. Training for and running a marathon with another person or group of people can make the experience more enjoyable and more rewarding. A running partner might be just the motivation you need to show up for an early morning run instead of rolling over to hit the snooze button. And, when you cross the finish line together, you can share the satisfaction of reaching your common goal.

Usually, thousands of people sign up and run a marathon. Most people finish the race. The thrill of running a marathon for the first time is unbelievable. The training sessions are harder if you have never run before. But it is unbelievable what ones' body can do when one puts their mind to it. Having a good coach to support you makes all the difference in training for a marathon.

The daily runs are very important. Strength training and core training are also very important. The health benefits you gain from training are tremendous. Your core muscles grow stronger, and you will have tighter thighs and gluts. Your heart will be much stronger, and you can maintain lower cholesterol and blood sugar levels. Overall, you will look better and become healthier.

Nothing can explain how people feel when they reach that finish line at the end of the race. All the hard work and months of training feel worthwhile. The feeling of accomplishing something great overtakes you. It is great to run a marathon, but it is even greater to finish it.

7. In what point of view is the below sentence said?
Many runners try to beat their own best time.

- Ⓐ first person
- Ⓑ second person
- Ⓒ third person
- Ⓓ third person limited

8. Which point of view is the following excerpt told from?

From Chapter 1 of **Bullets and Billets** by Bruce Bainsfather

I stood in a queue of Gordons, Seaforths, Worcesters, etc., slowly moving up one, until, finally arriving at the companion (nearly said staircase), I tobogganed down into the hold, and spent what was left of the night dealing out those rations. Having finished, at last, I came to the surface again, and now, as the transport glided along through the dirty waters of the river, and as I gazed at the motley collection of Frenchmen on the various wharves, and saw a variety of soldiery, and a host of other warlike "props," I felt acutely that now I was in the war at last—the real thing! For some time, I had been rehearsing in England; but that was over now, and here I was—in the common or garden vernacular—"in the soup."

- Ⓐ first person
- Ⓑ third person omniscient
- Ⓒ third person limited
- Ⓓ second person

Question 9 is based on the passage below

You read a research study that says eating a candy bar made of dark chocolate every day is good for your heart in the long run. The study followed the health of a large group of people over the course of ten years. You notice in fine print at the end of the research that the study was conducted by a major chocolate company.

9. What might you, as a critical reader, take away from this?

- Ⓐ The study must be true if it is published.
- Ⓑ The conductors of the study benefit from the findings of this claim.
- Ⓒ Before believing this to be true, more studies need to be done by people who don't have stakes in the particular market.
- Ⓓ both B and C

10. What is the author's purpose for writing the statement below?

If you are thinking about buying a new car, Bruce's on Route 12 has the best deals in town.

- Ⓐ to inform
- Ⓑ to instruct
- Ⓒ to sell
- Ⓓ to entertain

11. Often when reading a magazine you will come across advertisements. These advertisements are meant to:

- Ⓐ show the reader a product
- Ⓑ persuade the reader to buy the product
- Ⓒ introduce the reader to the product
- Ⓓ provide the reader with a break from stories

Test ID	8E020
Test Name	**Publishing Mediums**
Student Name	
Date	

1	Ⓐ Ⓑ Ⓒ Ⓓ	6	Ⓐ Ⓑ Ⓒ Ⓓ	11	Ⓐ Ⓑ Ⓒ Ⓓ	
2	Ⓐ Ⓑ Ⓒ Ⓓ	7	Ⓐ Ⓑ Ⓒ Ⓓ			
3	Ⓐ Ⓑ Ⓒ Ⓓ	8	Ⓐ Ⓑ Ⓒ Ⓓ			
4	Ⓐ Ⓑ Ⓒ Ⓓ	9	Ⓐ Ⓑ Ⓒ Ⓓ			
5	Ⓐ Ⓑ Ⓒ Ⓓ	10	Ⓐ Ⓑ Ⓒ Ⓓ			

Chapter 2 → Lesson 7: Publishing Mediums

1. **Which of the following is important to consider when reading a text online?**

   Ⓐ evaluate the background of the source
   Ⓑ look for why the information is being provided
   Ⓒ check the date of the source
   Ⓓ all of the above

2. **You want to write a short piece that people can respond to immediately and publicly. What is the best place to do this?**

   Ⓐ a web page
   Ⓑ the local newspaper
   Ⓒ the national newspaper
   Ⓓ a magazine

3. **You are writing an article about the stresses involved in being a high school student and what to do about them. What is the best medium/media of publication?**

   Ⓐ a magazine for teenagers
   Ⓑ a website aimed at teenagers
   Ⓒ a national newspaper
   Ⓓ both A and B

4. **What is the best way to learn about WWII?**

   Ⓐ to watch movies
   Ⓑ read nonfiction texts
   Ⓒ read first-hand accounts published online
   Ⓓ all of the above

5. **You want to create a literary analysis of two novels. What is the best way to present this information?**

   Ⓐ in print
   Ⓑ electronically
   Ⓒ with pictures
   Ⓓ online

6. **Your teacher tells you that you must show a visual representation of a scene from a popular book. What is the best way to do this?**

    Ⓐ a movie
    Ⓑ a play
    Ⓒ an article
    Ⓓ both A and B

7. **You want to ensure you will have as few problems as possible when presenting information for your final project. What medium of publication would be best to use?**

    Ⓐ use print
    Ⓑ use electronics
    Ⓒ with pictures
    Ⓓ power point

8. **You are writing a piece on your family's history that you would like your family in the country and in Europe to read and respond to as quickly as possible. What is the best way to do this?**

    Ⓐ to write them letters and enclose the information in the letter
    Ⓑ to create a webpage for them to visit
    Ⓒ to write the history electronically and email it to them
    Ⓓ either B or C

9. **You want to persuade students in your school to vote for you in the upcoming student government elections. What medium of publication would be best to do this?**

    Ⓐ in your school newspaper
    Ⓑ in your local newspaper
    Ⓒ on a website
    Ⓓ through a slide show

10. **What is the best place to search for a specific recipe you need in a hurry?**

    Ⓐ Internet
    Ⓑ magazine
    Ⓒ newspaper
    Ⓓ recipe books

11. If your dad wants to learn how to operate a paint sprayer correctly, where is the best place to look?

Ⓐ magazines
Ⓑ Internet
Ⓒ book
Ⓓ none of these.

Test ID	8E021
Test Name	**Evaluating Authors Claims**
Student Name	
Date	

1	(A) (B) (C) (D)	6	(A) (B) (C) (D)	11	Answer in the space provided below.
2	(A) (B) (C) (D)	7	(A) (B) (C) (D)	12	Answer in the space provided below.
3	(A) (B) (C) (D)	8	(A) (B) (C) (D)		
4	(A) (B) (C) (D)	9	(A) (B) (C) (D)		
5	(A) (B) (C) (D)	10	(A) (B) (C) (D) (E)		

11 ×
[   ]
                                                                    +

12 ×
[   ]
                                                                    +

Chapter 2 → Lesson 8: Evaluating Author Claims

1. What is an author's claim?

- Ⓐ his or her argument
- Ⓑ the support for his or her argument
- Ⓒ his or her opinion
- Ⓓ the facts for the argument

2. What evidence must you look at in evaluating an author's claim?

- Ⓐ the argument itself
- Ⓑ the support that the author provides to back up his or her argument
- Ⓒ the author's opinion about that which he or she is arguing
- Ⓓ how many people support the argument.

3. What is the best way to determine the accuracy of evidence provided by the author?

- Ⓐ ask somebody
- Ⓑ personal experience
- Ⓒ look it up on the computer, any site will do
- Ⓓ do your own research

4. Which of the following is the least acceptable piece of evidence?

- Ⓐ statistics
- Ⓑ quotes taken from a reliable source
- Ⓒ opinion
- Ⓓ facts

5. Emotional appeals (appealing to the reader's emotions) should...

- Ⓐ never be used
- Ⓑ be used sometimes
- Ⓒ should always be used
- Ⓓ none of the above

6. The author's evidence must...

- Ⓐ partially support the author's claims
- Ⓑ always be taken from a primary source
- Ⓒ directly support the author's claims
- Ⓓ all of the above

7. Which of the following should you look at when examining the author's claim?

Ⓐ What is the author's purpose?
Ⓑ What are the sources that the author has cited?
Ⓒ Does the author provide evidence several times in the passage to strengthen his claim?
Ⓓ What is the purpose of the evidence?

Question 8-10 are based on the passage below

The Necessity of Exercise

(1) 58 million Americans are overweight (getfitamerica.com). (2) This number is and has been on a steady rise. More and more Americans are exercising less and less. (3) The Center for Disease Control recommends 2.5 hours of moderate aerobic activity each week, along with 2 days of strength training. (4) Americans are clearly not abiding by these minimum recommendations as the numbers prove. (5) It is necessary for Americans to get more exercise in order to lead healthy lives. (6) There is no good reason for healthy people not to exercise, but there are many benefits, including maintaining a healthy weight, relieving everyday stress and lowering one's chances for certain diseases.

8. Which of the sentences above includes the author's argument?

Ⓐ 3
Ⓑ 4
Ⓒ 5
Ⓓ 6

9. According to the author's introduction, what are the points that provide evidence?

Ⓐ how much exercise people need
Ⓑ how much exercise one needs to maintain a healthy weight
Ⓒ how exercise raises everyday stress
Ⓓ how exercise increases risk for certain diseases

10. Which of the author's statements provides evidence?

Ⓐ 1
Ⓑ 2
Ⓒ 3
Ⓓ 4
Ⓔ 5

11. Determine whether the following statement is a fact, supported opinion, or unsupported opinion:

   Texas is the hottest state in the United States.

   Write your answer in the box given below.

   ┌───┐
   │   │
   │   │
   │   │
   └───┘

12. Determine whether the following statement is a fact, supported opinion, or unsupported opinion.

   Smoking should not be allowed in public places because second hand smoke is dangerous. Write your answer in the box given below.

   ┌───┐
   │   │
   │   │
   │   │
   └───┘

Test ID	8E022
Test Name	**Conflicting Information**
Student Name	
Date	

1	Ⓐ Ⓑ Ⓒ Ⓓ	**6**	Ⓐ Ⓑ
2	Ⓐ Ⓑ	**7**	Answer in the space provided below.
3	Ⓐ Ⓑ	**8**	Answer in the space provided below.
4	Ⓐ Ⓑ	**9**	Ⓐ Ⓑ Ⓒ Ⓓ
5	Ⓐ Ⓑ Ⓒ Ⓓ	**10**	Ⓐ Ⓑ Ⓒ

7

×

+

8

×

+

Chapter 2 → Lesson 9: Conflicting Information

1. When you come across two conflicting viewpoints, what should you do?

   Ⓐ research other sources to find out which fact is correct
   Ⓑ look to see if the fact may have changed
   Ⓒ examine the reliability of both writers
   Ⓓ all of the above

2. Determine whether the writers are presenting conflicting information based on fact or interpretation.

   Writer One: Geology is a branch of science.
   Writer Two: Geology is a branch of math.

   Ⓐ fact
   Ⓑ opinion

3. Determine whether the writers are presenting conflicting information based on fact or interpretation.

   Writer One: The president's sweater was too small.
   Writer Two: The president's sweater fit him well.

   Ⓐ fact
   Ⓑ opinion

4. Determine whether the writers are presenting conflicting information based on fact or interpretation.

   Writer One: The worst storm of the season passed through Seattle yesterday.
   Writer Two: A moderate storm passed through Seattle yesterday.

   Ⓐ fact
   Ⓑ opinion

5. Which of the following is an example of a fact that could change?

   Ⓐ someone's name
   Ⓑ the location of a store
   Ⓒ the area of a park
   Ⓓ all of the above

6. Determine whether the conflicting information presented by the two authors is fact or interpretation.

Einstein
Albert Einstein was born on March 14th, 1879, in the German city of Ulm, without any indication that he was destined for greatness.

Einstein
Albert Einstein was born on March 15, 1879, in the city of Ulm. When he was born, people did not think he was going to be anything special.

Ⓐ   fact
Ⓑ   interpretation

7. Determine whether the following is fact or opinion.

Bailey is wearing blue shoes.

Write your answer in the box given below.

8. Determine whether the following is fact or opinion.

Dr. Blair studied at the most prestigious of schools, Harvard University.

Write your answer in the box given below.

9. Which of the following is not a reason for the differing interpretations between texts?

    Ⓐ The authors are trying to prove different points.
    Ⓑ One or both of the authors may be trying to persuade the reader to believe one way.
    Ⓒ The authors are both trying to be objective.
    Ⓓ Subjectivity is often apparent in writing.

10. Determine whether the following is fact or opinion.

    The atrocious painting sold for $1,000,000.

    Ⓐ fact
    Ⓑ opinion
    Ⓒ both

End of Reading Informational Text

Chapter 3
Language

Test ID	8E023
Test Name	**Adjectives and Adverbs**
Student Name	
Date	

1	Ⓐ Ⓑ Ⓒ Ⓓ	6	Ⓐ Ⓑ Ⓒ Ⓓ	11	Answer in the space provided below.
2	Ⓐ Ⓑ Ⓒ Ⓓ	7	Ⓐ Ⓑ Ⓒ Ⓓ	12	Answer in the space provided below.
3	Ⓐ Ⓑ Ⓒ Ⓓ	8	Ⓐ Ⓑ Ⓒ Ⓓ	13	Answer in the space provided below.
4	Ⓐ Ⓑ Ⓒ Ⓓ	9	Ⓐ Ⓑ Ⓒ Ⓓ	14	Answer in the space provided below.
5	Ⓐ Ⓑ Ⓒ Ⓓ	10	Ⓐ Ⓑ Ⓒ Ⓓ	15	Answer in the space provided below.
				16	Answer in the space provided below.

11

12

13

14

15

16

Lesson 1: Adjectives and Adverbs

1. What is an adjective?

Ⓐ a word that modifies (describes) a verb
Ⓑ a word that modifies (describes) a noun in a sentence
Ⓒ a word that modifies (describes) a sentence
Ⓓ a word that modifies (describes) descriptive words

2. What is an adverb?

Ⓐ a word that modifies (describes) adjectives
Ⓑ a word that modifies (describes) verbs
Ⓒ a word that modifies (describes) adverbs
Ⓓ a word that modifies (describes) descriptive words

3. A lot of people have trouble with the words "good" and "well". See if you can use them correctly in the following sentences by choosing the correct words in correct sequence.

a) I am _____.
b) Dinner was really _____ .
c) They are _____ baseball players.
d) You play really_____.

Ⓐ well, well, good, good
Ⓑ well, good, well, good
Ⓒ well, good, good, good
Ⓓ well, good, good, well

4. Choose the correct adjective/ adverb sequence for the following sentences.

a) I stayed home from school because when I woke up this morning I felt (bad/ badly).
b) I did (good/ well) on my science test.
c) I answered the question as (honest/ honestly) as I could.

Ⓐ bad, good, honest
Ⓑ badly, well, honestly
Ⓒ bad, well, honestly
Ⓓ badly, well, honestly

5. Which choice is the adverb that correctly completes the following sentence?

I am very fond of Miss Jenkins; she teaches very _____.

Ⓐ patiently
Ⓑ patient
Ⓒ patience
Ⓓ patiented

6. Which word is the adverb in the following sentence?

She picked up the sweet baby very carefully.

Ⓐ sweet
Ⓑ very
Ⓒ carefully
Ⓓ both B and C

7. Which word in the following sentence is an adjective?

After a long afternoon at practice, I am tired, hungry, and dirty.

Ⓐ tired
Ⓑ hungry
Ⓒ dirty
Ⓓ all of the above

8. What is the adjective in the following sentence?

The pretty girl brushed her hair before she went to bed.

Ⓐ pretty
Ⓑ girl
Ⓒ brushed
Ⓓ hair

9. What is the adverb in the following sentence?

He slowly walked towards the elevator on his floor.

Ⓐ slowly
Ⓑ elevator
Ⓒ floor
Ⓓ walked

10. What is the adverb in the following sentence?

Jimmy sadly walked away after having lost a tough game of baseball.

- Ⓐ sadly
- Ⓑ lost
- Ⓒ tough
- Ⓓ baseball

11. What is the adjective in the following sentence?

Greg bounced around the playground, happily playing on his new slide.

Write your answer in the box given below.

12. What is the adverb in the following sentence?

Greg bounced around the playground, happily playing on his new slide.

Write your answer in the box given below.

13. What is the adjective in the following sentence?

Bob's mother laughed when she saw her blonde son lazily lounging by the pool.

Write your answer in the box given below.

14. What is the adverb in the following sentence?

Bob's mother laughed when she saw her blonde son lazily lounging by the pool.

Write your answer in the box given below.

15. What is the adjective in the following sentence?

Although her husband claims their dog is one of the smartest breeds, Caroline was fairly certain he is mistaken.

Write your answer in the box given below.

16. What is the adverb in the following sentence?

Although her husband claims their dog is one of the smartest breeds, Caroline was fairly certain he is mistaken.

Write your answer in the box given below.

Test ID	8E024
Test Name	**Subject-Verb Agreement**
Student Name	
Date	

1	Ⓐ Ⓑ Ⓒ Ⓓ	6	Ⓐ Ⓑ Ⓒ Ⓓ	11	Answer in the space provided below.
2	Ⓐ Ⓑ	7	Ⓐ Ⓑ Ⓒ Ⓓ	12	Answer in the space provided below.
3	Ⓐ Ⓑ Ⓒ Ⓓ	8	Ⓐ Ⓑ Ⓒ		
4	Ⓐ Ⓑ Ⓒ Ⓓ	9	Ⓐ Ⓑ Ⓒ Ⓓ		
5	Ⓐ Ⓑ Ⓒ Ⓓ	10	Ⓐ Ⓑ Ⓒ Ⓓ		

11 ×
[   ]
+

12 ×
[   ]
+

Chapter 3 → Lesson 2: Subject-Verb Agreement

1. Select the correct verb form to agree with the subject in the following sentence.

Either the teacher or the principal _____ going to contact you.

  (A) are
  (B) is
  (C) not
  (D) never

2. Which sentence shows the correct subject-verb agreement?

  a) Neither the cat nor the dogs have been fed.
  b) Neither the cat nor the dogs has been fed.

  (A) a
  (B) b

3. Select the correct verb form to agree with the subject in the following sentence.

_____ my sister or my parents going to pick me up?

  (A) Is
  (B) Are
  (C) you're
  (D) watching

4. Select the correct verb form to agree with the subject in the following sentence.

Some of the answers _____ to have been wrong.

  (A) seems
  (B) seem
  (C) just
  (D) really

5. Select the correct verb form to agree with the subject in the following sentence.

Mary and Joe _____ going to the dance together.

  (A) is
  (B) are
  (C) wouldn't
  (D) walking

6. Select the correct verb form to agree with the subject in the following sentence.

The highlighter or the marker _____ in the side drawer.

Ⓐ is
Ⓑ are
Ⓒ rolling
Ⓓ writing

7. Select the correct verb form to agree with the subject in the following sentence.

The student, along with his parents, _____ coming to the talent show.

Ⓐ is
Ⓑ are
Ⓒ never
Ⓓ walking

8. Select the correct verb form to agree with the subject in the following sentence.

Neither the tomatoes nor the mint in my garden _____ begun to grow.

Ⓐ has
Ⓑ have
Ⓒ it doesn't matter which verb form is used

9. Identify the subject(s) in the following sentence.

Some of the food is spoiled because it was sitting in the sun too long.

Ⓐ The food
Ⓑ some and food
Ⓒ sitting in the sun
Ⓓ food is spoiled

10. Identify the subject(s) in the following sentence.

Either the teacher or the principal is going to contact you regarding your grades.

Ⓐ either the teacher
Ⓑ contact you
Ⓒ Either the teacher or the principal
Ⓓ regarding your grades

11. Fill in the blank with the correct verb.

The boys and girls _____ very excited about the trip next week.

12. Fill in the blank with the correct verb.

The boys and Sally _____ going skiing together.

Test ID	8E025
Test Name	Pronouns
Student Name	
Date	

1	Ⓐ Ⓑ Ⓒ Ⓓ	6	Ⓐ Ⓑ	11	Answer in the space provided below.
2	Ⓐ Ⓑ Ⓒ Ⓓ	7	Ⓐ Ⓑ	12	Answer in the space provided below.
3	Ⓐ Ⓑ Ⓒ Ⓓ	8	Ⓐ Ⓑ Ⓒ Ⓓ		
4	Ⓐ Ⓑ Ⓒ Ⓓ	9	Ⓐ Ⓑ Ⓒ Ⓓ		
5	Ⓐ Ⓑ	10	Ⓐ Ⓑ Ⓒ Ⓓ		

11

12

Chapter 3 → Lesson 3: Pronouns

1. Select the pronoun that will best fit into the following sentence.

The instructor put _____ students at ease when he said no one would fail.

- Ⓐ we
- Ⓑ his
- Ⓒ their
- Ⓓ them

2. Select the pronoun that will best fit into the following sentence.

My grandmother and _____ enjoyed spending the day together at the fair.

- Ⓐ I
- Ⓑ myself
- Ⓒ me
- Ⓓ my

3. Select the pronoun that will best fit into the following sentence.

_____ students laughed so loudly that the class next door was distracted from their lesson.

- Ⓐ We
- Ⓑ Us
- Ⓒ Them
- Ⓓ Those

4. To what does the demonstrative pronoun "that" refer to in the following sentences?

I saw a terrible skateboarding accident down the street. That was awful.

- Ⓐ The skateboarding accident
- Ⓑ Being in the street
- Ⓒ Seeing the skateboard down the street
- Ⓓ The awful thing

5. Choose the correct pronoun in the sentence below.

The woman (who/whom) is wearing the red dress would like to make a reservation.

- Ⓐ who
- Ⓑ whom

6. Choose the correct pronoun in the sentence below.

With (who/whom) were you speaking?

Ⓐ who
Ⓑ whom

7. Choose the correct pronoun in the sentence below.

(Who/whom) can you send to help us?

Ⓐ who
Ⓑ whom

8. Identify the pronoun in the following sentence.

Martha's sister wanted her siblings to give her something exciting for her birthday.

Ⓐ Martha
Ⓑ sister
Ⓒ birthday
Ⓓ her

9. To what does the demonstrative pronoun "those" refer to in the following sentences?

Since I was going to be carting furniture up and downstairs, I put on my favorite pair of shoes. My daughter looked me over once and said, "You're wearing those?"

Ⓐ the shirt
Ⓑ the shoes
Ⓒ the shorts
Ⓓ the whole look

10. Identify the pronoun in the following sentence.

Mike's mother told him that the trash needed to be taken out sooner rather than later.

Ⓐ Mike
Ⓑ mother
Ⓒ him
Ⓓ trash

11. Fill in the blank with the correct pronoun:

Julie couldn't believe _____ friend didn't listen to _____ advice.

12. Fill in the blank with the correct pronouns:

Michael noticed that _____ buddy was wearing the same shirt as _____.

Test ID	8E026
Test Name	**Phrases and Clauses**
Student Name	
Date	

1	(A) (B) (C) (D)	6	(A) (B) (C) (D)	11	Answer in the space provided below.
2	Answer in the space provided below.	7	(A) (B) (C) (D)		
3	(A) (B)	8	(A) (B) (C) (D)		
4	(A) (B)	9	(A) (B)		
5	(A) (B)	10	(A) (B) (C) (D)		

×

2 [   ]

+

×

11 [   ]

+

Chapter 3 → Lesson 4: Phrases and Clauses

1. Which of the following sentences is an infinitive phrase?

Ⓐ To make my birthday special, my family threw me a surprise party.
Ⓑ My teacher, the one wearing the blue dress, gave us our final yesterday.
Ⓒ Mary waited at the bus stop, hoping another would come by.
Ⓓ On the side of the road, we saw a perfectly good couch.

2. Identify whether the following is an independent or subordinate clause.

The boy cried.

3. Identify whether the following is an independent or subordinate clause.

When I jumped down

Ⓐ independent
Ⓑ subordinate

4. Identify whether the following is an independent or subordinate clause.

He stopped.

Ⓐ independent
Ⓑ subordinate

5. Identify whether the following is an independent or subordinate clause:

If he had run

Ⓐ independent
Ⓑ subordinate

6. What is an independent clause?

Ⓐ It has a subject and verb and can be a complete sentence by itself.
Ⓑ It has a subject and a verb but cannot stand by itself as a complete sentence.
Ⓒ It is only part of a sentence.
Ⓓ It does not have either a subject or a verb and is therefore not a sentence.

7. What is a subordinate clause?

Ⓐ It has a subject and verb and can be a complete sentence by itself.
Ⓑ It has a subject and a verb but cannot stand by itself as a complete sentence.
Ⓒ It is only two words.
Ⓓ It does not have either a subject or a verb and is therefore not a sentence.

8. What is an adjective phrase?

Ⓐ It modifies a noun.
Ⓑ It modifies a verb, adverb, or adjective.
Ⓒ It tells "what kind" or "which one".
Ⓓ both A and C

9. What does the following sentence contain?

The dog with the bright blue collar jumped on me.

Ⓐ an adverb phrase
Ⓑ an adjective phrase

10. Identify the type of phrase in the following sentence.

Because she did not clean her room, Bethany lost her iPad privileges for the weekend.

Ⓐ adjective
Ⓑ adverb
Ⓒ gerund
Ⓓ noun

11. Is the clause in the following sentence independent or subordinate?

My son, an accomplished fisherman, caught the largest fish in the tournament.

Test ID	8E027
Test Name	Verbals
Student Name	
Date	

1	Ⓐ Ⓑ Ⓒ Ⓓ	6	Ⓐ Ⓑ Ⓒ Ⓓ	11	Ⓐ Ⓑ Ⓒ
2	Ⓐ Ⓑ Ⓒ Ⓓ	7	Ⓐ Ⓑ Ⓒ Ⓓ	12	Ⓐ Ⓑ Ⓒ
3	Ⓐ Ⓑ Ⓒ Ⓓ	8	Ⓐ Ⓑ Ⓒ Ⓓ		
4	Ⓐ Ⓑ Ⓒ Ⓓ	9	Ⓐ Ⓑ Ⓒ Ⓓ		
5	Ⓐ Ⓑ Ⓒ Ⓓ	10	Ⓐ Ⓑ Ⓒ Ⓓ		

Chapter 3 → Lesson 5: Verbals

1. What is the definition of a verbal?

Ⓐ a spoken form of communication
Ⓑ forms of verbs that function as other parts of speech
Ⓒ a very descriptive word
Ⓓ a word that contains a sound

2. Which verbals function as adjectives?

Ⓐ infinitives
Ⓑ participles
Ⓒ gerunds
Ⓓ nouns

3. Which verbals function as nouns?

Ⓐ infinitives
Ⓑ gerunds
Ⓒ participles
Ⓓ verbs

4. Which verbals function as nouns, adjectives, or adverbials?

Ⓐ gerunds
Ⓑ infinitives
Ⓒ participles
Ⓓ verbs

5. Which of the following sentences uses the verbal known as an infinitive?

Ⓐ Looking back through the photo albums gives me fond memories of the time I spent in Italy with my grandparents.
Ⓑ My cousins like to visit the beach when they come to our house, since they live in the mountains.
Ⓒ She was terminated from her job because she was never on time.
Ⓓ Kelsey received the best present for her birthday

6. Which of the following sentences uses the verbal known as a gerund?

Ⓐ Sarah enjoys hiking on the local trails.
Ⓑ My older sister is going to go off to college at the end of summer.
Ⓒ I really enjoy giving special gifts to my friends and family members on their birthdays.
Ⓓ My favorite time of the year is summer vacation.

7. Which of the following sentences uses the verbal known as a participle?

  Ⓐ After school, my friends and I are going to go to the mall.
  Ⓑ The soup boiling on the stove smells delicious.
  Ⓒ I walked my dog around the block.
  Ⓓ My friends are coming over after school today.

8. What part of speech is the verbal taking in the following sentence?

The sparkling ring is beautiful.

  Ⓐ noun
  Ⓑ adjective
  Ⓒ verb
  Ⓓ adverb

9. What part of speech is the verbal taking in the following sentence?

The bird was sleeping in its nest.

  Ⓐ noun
  Ⓑ adjective
  Ⓒ verb
  Ⓓ adverb

10. What part of speech is the verbal taking in the following sentence?

The sound of running water became louder and louder.

  Ⓐ noun
  Ⓑ adjective
  Ⓒ verb
  Ⓓ adverb

11. What part of speech is the verbal taking in the following sentence?

Jogging is my least favorite cardio activity.

Ⓐ noun
Ⓑ adjective
Ⓒ adverbial

12. What part of speech is the verbal taking in the following sentence?

The laughing children were having a fabulous time on the Ferris wheel.

Ⓐ noun
Ⓑ adjective
Ⓒ verb

Test ID	8E028
Test Name	Capitalization
Student Name	
Date	

1	Ⓐ Ⓑ Ⓒ Ⓓ	6	Ⓐ Ⓑ Ⓒ Ⓓ	11	Answer in the space provided below.
2	Ⓐ Ⓑ Ⓒ Ⓓ	7	Ⓐ Ⓑ Ⓒ Ⓓ	12	Answer in the space provided below.
3	Ⓐ Ⓑ Ⓒ Ⓓ	8	Ⓐ Ⓑ Ⓒ Ⓓ		
4	Ⓐ Ⓑ Ⓒ Ⓓ	9	Ⓐ Ⓑ Ⓒ Ⓓ		
5	Ⓐ Ⓑ Ⓒ Ⓓ	10	Ⓐ Ⓑ		

11 ×
[   ]
+

12 ×
[   ]
+

Chapter 3 → Lesson 6: Capitalization

1. Which of the following words should always be capitalized?

Ⓐ Grandmother
Ⓑ the first word of every sentence
Ⓒ names of subjects, such as Science
Ⓓ all of the above

2. What is the correct way to capitalize "grandmother" in the below sentences?

a. We should go visit (grandmother/ Grandmother) today.
b. This weekend we went to see my (grandmother/ Grandmother).

Ⓐ grandmother, grandmother
Ⓑ Grandmother, grandmother
Ⓒ grandmother, Grandmother
Ⓓ None of the above

3. Which words need to be capitalized in the following sentences?

next week, my report on wwll is due. I have an awful lot of studying and research to complete; it looks like I will be spending a lot of time at the Joann Darcy public library.

Ⓐ next
Ⓑ wwll
Ⓒ public library
Ⓓ all of the above

4. How many capitalization errors are in the following passage?

Every morning I have the same routine. First, i make my bed and fluff my pillows. Next, i head to the shower. I always pick my clothes out the night before so that I don't spend too much time on deciding what to wear. Then, I run downstairs to eat cheerios, my favorite cereal, and finally, I brush my teeth. On the way out of the door, I grab my backpack, which hangs on a hook by the front door, and hug my mom goodbye before I rush off to meet the bus.

Ⓐ 2
Ⓑ 3
Ⓒ 4
Ⓓ none

5. Which of the following must always be capitalized?

Ⓐ names of states
Ⓑ names of seasons
Ⓒ every word in the title of a work of literature
Ⓓ none of the above

6. Which of the following are always capitalized?

Ⓐ names of holidays
Ⓑ languages
Ⓒ days of the week
Ⓓ all of the above

7. Which of the following sentences contains a capitalization error?

Ⓐ I can't wait for Spring!
Ⓑ Spring has finally arrived.
Ⓒ I titled my narrative, The Best Spring Break Ever.
Ⓓ None of the above.

8. Which is the correct way to capitalize the word, "mayor" in a sentence?

Ⓐ This weekend, I had the opportunity to meet Mayor Sandburg of Gantsville.
Ⓑ This weekend, I had the opportunity to meet Carl Sandburg, the mayor of Gantsville.
Ⓒ Both of the above.
Ⓓ None of the above.

9. Which is the correct way to capitalize the abbreviation for the state of California?

Ⓐ Ca
Ⓑ Calif
Ⓒ CA
Ⓓ Cali

10. Is it correct to capitalize the first letter of a quote when it is in the middle of a sentence, as in the following example?

Samuel Montgomery once said, "Every once in a while we must evaluate ourselves, for only with self reflection can we reach perfection."

Ⓐ Yes
Ⓑ No

11. Which word should be capitalized in the following sentence?

Betty and I are going to france for spring break.
Write your answer in the box given below.

```
┌─────────────────────────────────────────┐
│                                         │
│                                         │
│                                         │
└─────────────────────────────────────────┘
```

12. What should be capitalized in the following sentence?

One of my favorite plays is romeo and juliet.
Write your answer in the box given below.

```
┌─────────────────────────────────────────┐
│                                         │
│                                         │
│                                         │
└─────────────────────────────────────────┘
```

Test ID	8E029
Test Name	**Punctuation**
Student Name	
Date	

1	(A) (B) (C) (D)	6	(A) (B) (C) (D)
2	(A) (B) (C) (D)	7	(A) (B) (C) (D)
3	(A) (B) (C) (D)	8	(A) (B) (C) (D)
4	(A) (B) (C) (D)	9	Answer in the space provided below.
5	(A) (B) (C) (D)	10	Answer in the space provided below.

9

10

Chapter 3 → Lesson 7: Punctuation

1. Determine which sentence shows the correct usage of the comma.

Ⓐ Please pick up glue, scissors, and construction paper.
Ⓑ The names of my pets are, Max, Goldie, and Emily.
Ⓒ I looked everywhere for my keys, including the trash and under the couch and in the kitchen.
Ⓓ My father Jim and my mother Martha enjoy camping dancing and jogging together.

2. The following sentences is missing one or more commas. Determine which example shows the correct comma placement.

Ⓐ My uncle, who is an incredibly talented actor encouraged me to try out in the talent show.
Ⓑ My uncle who is an incredibly talented actor, encouraged me to try out in the talent show.
Ⓒ My uncle, who is an incredibly talented actor, encouraged me to try out for the talent show.
Ⓓ My uncle who, is an incredibly talented actor, encouraged me to try out for the talent show.

3. How would you fix the following sentence?

After you have finished taking out the trash you may watch your favorite show.

Ⓐ After you have finished, taking out the trash you may watch your favorite show.
Ⓑ After you have finished taking out the trash, you may watch your favorite show.
Ⓒ After, you have finished taking out the trash you may watch your favorite show.
Ⓓ After you have finished taking out the trash you may watch your favorite show.

4. Select the sentence that shows the correct usage of the semicolon.

Ⓐ Her uncle is coming to visit; and he is traveling from far away.
Ⓑ This summer we went camping; always fun.
Ⓒ I enjoy the arts; I especially love to paint with watercolors.
Ⓓ I enjoy the arts and; I especially love to paint with watercolors.

5. Determine which sentence shows the correct usage of the apostrophe.

Ⓐ That girl is Mrs. Jones's daughter.
Ⓑ That girl is Mrs. Jones' daughter.
Ⓒ That girl is Mrs. Jones daughter.
Ⓓ That girl is Mrs'. Jones' daughter.

6. Which of the following is the plural possessive form of "mice"?

Ⓐ mices
Ⓑ mices'
Ⓒ mice's
Ⓓ mouse's

7. Determine which sentence shows the correct usage of the apostrophe and comma.

Ⓐ I couldn't wait to see Katie's new dog, Alfie.
Ⓑ I couldn't wait to see Katies new dog, Alfie.
Ⓒ I couldn't wait to see Katie new dog Alfie.
Ⓓ I couldn't wait to see Katie's new dog Alfie.

8. Which of the following does the contraction "would've" take the place of?

Ⓐ would of
Ⓑ would have
Ⓒ will of
Ⓓ will have

9. What is the best way to fix the following sentence?

Yvettes invitation for Brendas surprise party said to bring the following things to the party cupcakes soda and a gag gift

10. Where would you include a dash in the following sentence?

Kasey had not taken the time to read the directions no wonder the bookcase fell apart after an hour!

Test ID	8E030
Test Name	Ellipsis
Student Name	
Date	

1	(A) (B) (C) (D)	6	(A) (B)	
2	(A) (B) (C) (D)	7	(A) (B) (C) (D)	
3	(A) (B)	8	(A) (B) (C) (D)	
4	(A) (B)	9	(A) (B)	
5	(A) (B)	10	(A) (B) (C) (D)	

Chapter 3 → Lesson 8: Ellipsis

1. Which of the following symbols is an ellipsis?

- Ⓐ ...
- Ⓑ ;
- Ⓒ :
- Ⓓ --

2. What is the purpose of an ellipsis?

- Ⓐ To indicate text has been omitted
- Ⓑ To add extra significance to sentence
- Ⓒ To end sentence powerfully
- Ⓓ Both A and B

3. An ellipsis can be used to create suspense.

- Ⓐ True
- Ⓑ False

4. You cannot use an ellipsis at the beginning of a sentence.

- Ⓐ True
- Ⓑ False

5. If an ellipsis comes at the end of the sentence, add it after the period for a total of 4 dots, so it looks like this....
Mark "True" or "False"

- Ⓐ True
- Ⓑ False

6. The following is the correct use of an ellipsis.
I don't know...I'm not sure...What do you think?
Mark "True" or "False"

- Ⓐ True
- Ⓑ False

7. When is it appropriate to use an ellipsis?

- Ⓐ when citing evidence from a text that is long
- Ⓑ when researching and information is at the beginning and end of a paragraph
- Ⓒ when trying to be concise and only use necessary facts
- Ⓓ all of the above

8. What is the appropriate way to cite the following information?

58 million Americans are overweight (getfitamerica.com). This number is and has been on a steady rise. More and more Americans are exercising less and less. The Center for Disease Control recommends 2.5 hours of moderate aerobic activity each week, along with 2 days of strength training. Americans are clearly not abiding by these minimum recommendations as the numbers prove. It is necessary for Americans to get more exercise in order to lead a healthy life. There is no good reason for healthy people not to exercise but there are many benefits including maintaining a healthy weight, relieving everyday stress and lowering one's chances for certain diseases.

Ⓐ After examining the facts, it is evident that Americans need exercise. A recent article explained, "58 million Americans are overweight-- It is necessary for Americans to get more exercise in order to lead a healthy life."

Ⓑ After examining the facts, it is evident that Americans need exercise. A recent article explained, "58 million Americans are overweight: It is necessary for Americans to get more exercise in order to lead a healthy life."

Ⓒ After examining the facts, it is evident that Americans need exercise. A recent article explained, "58 million Americans are overweight… It is necessary for Americans to get more exercise in order to lead a healthy life."

Ⓓ None of the above

9. The following sentence properly uses an ellipsis?

"…[T]here are many benefits including maintaining a healthy weight, relieving everyday stress and lowering one's chances for certain diseases."

Ⓐ True
Ⓑ False

10. What is the appropriate way to cite the following information?

It was a dark and stormy night. The people of Cape Hatteras hid indoors. Mrs. Peabody shivered, hoping the hurricane would not visit and wondering whether she would be able to fall asleep. Across the street, Mr. Greer kept watch from the high tower of his attic, certain that the hurricane would strike soon.

Ⓐ The newspaper reported on the hurricane. The writer explained, "The people of Cape Hatteras hid indoors. … Mr. Greer kept watch from the high tower of his attic…."

Ⓑ The newspaper reported on the hurricane. The writer explained, "The people of Cape Hatteras hid indoors; Mr. Greer kept watch from the high tower of his attic…."

Ⓒ The newspaper reported on the hurricane. The writer explained, "The people of Cape Hatteras hid indoors. Mr. Greer kept watch from the high tower of his attic…."

Ⓓ None of the above

Test ID	8E031
Test Name	**Spelling**
Student Name	
Date	

1	Ⓐ Ⓑ Ⓒ Ⓓ	6	Ⓐ Ⓑ Ⓒ Ⓓ	11	Answer in the space provided below.
2	Ⓐ Ⓑ Ⓒ Ⓓ	7	Ⓐ Ⓑ Ⓒ Ⓓ	12	Answer in the space provided below.
3	Ⓐ Ⓑ Ⓒ Ⓓ	8	Ⓐ Ⓑ Ⓒ Ⓓ		
4	Ⓐ Ⓑ Ⓒ Ⓓ	9	Answer in the space provided below.		
5	Ⓐ Ⓑ Ⓒ Ⓓ	10	Ⓐ Ⓑ Ⓒ Ⓓ		

9 ×

+

11 ×

+

12 ×

+

Chapter 3 → Lesson 9: Spelling

1. What are homophones or homonyms?

Ⓐ the scientific name for humans
Ⓑ two or more words that are pronounced the same but have different meanings
Ⓒ two or more words that mean the opposite
Ⓓ none of the above

2. Choose the words that correctly complete the following sentence. Make sure that you pick the answer that shows the words in the correct sequence, as they would appear in the sentence.

I accidentally _____ the ball _____ the living room window.

Ⓐ through/ threw
Ⓑ threw/ though
Ⓒ threw/ through
Ⓓ through/through

3. Choose the words that correctly complete the following sentence. Make sure that you pick the answer that shows the words in the correct sequence, as they would appear in the sentence.

My cousins are so silly. _____ always running late because _____ are no alarm clocks in _____ house to wake them up in the morning.

Ⓐ There, they're, their
Ⓑ They're, there, their
Ⓒ Their, there, they're
Ⓓ There, there, there

4. Which word(s) in the following passage are misspelled?

I was trying to acommodate all of my friends. They were all coming to my birthday party, and I wanted to insure that I had the coolest prizes for the winners of the games; I made sure their were enough prizes for everyone.

Ⓐ acommodate
Ⓑ insure
Ⓒ their
Ⓓ all of the above

5. Which word(s) in the following passage are misspelled?

The night of the dance was amazing. My parents rented a limousine for my friends and me. When it pulled up, the chaufer held the door open for us and we climbed in, one after the other. We wore the fanciest dresses that we could find and wore the sparkliest accessories.

Ⓐ limousine
Ⓑ chaufer
Ⓒ sparkliest
Ⓓ accessories

6. What is the correct spelling for the misspelled or misused word in the sentence below?

I couldn't weight to go to the movies.

Ⓐ wait
Ⓑ wieght
Ⓒ moovies
Ⓓ moveis

7. What is the correct spelling for the misspelled word in the sentence below?

I had to write a buisness letter for English class.

Ⓐ right
Ⓑ business
Ⓒ bisness
Ⓓ no misspelled words

8. What is the correct spelling for the misspelled word in the sentence below?

Usually, I like to read on the beach; however, occationally I will swim.

Ⓐ usualy
Ⓑ beech
Ⓒ occasionally
Ⓓ no change

9. What is the correct spelling for the misspelled word in the sentence below?

I am going to perswade my mother to buy me a dog.

10. What is the correct spelling for the misspelled word in the sentence below?

It is unclear whether or not I will go on vacation with my family.

- Ⓐ weather
- Ⓑ knot
- Ⓒ vacetion
- Ⓓ none of the above

11. What is the correct spelling for the misspelled word in the sentence below?

My little brother can be such a nusssance when he is hungry for dinner.

Write the correct spelling in the box given below.

12. What is the correct spelling for the misspelled word in the sentence below?

Their is a loose dog in the neighborhood.

Write the correct spelling in the box given below.

Test ID	8E032
Test Name	**Mood in Verbs**
Student Name	
Date	

1	Ⓐ Ⓑ Ⓒ Ⓓ	6	Ⓐ Ⓑ Ⓒ Ⓓ
2	Ⓐ Ⓑ Ⓒ Ⓓ	7	Ⓐ Ⓑ Ⓒ Ⓓ
3	Ⓐ Ⓑ Ⓒ Ⓓ	8 A	Ⓐ Ⓑ Ⓒ Ⓓ
4	Ⓐ Ⓑ Ⓒ Ⓓ	8 B	Ⓐ Ⓑ Ⓒ Ⓓ
5	Ⓐ Ⓑ Ⓒ Ⓓ	9	Ⓐ Ⓑ Ⓒ Ⓓ

Chapter 3 → Lesson 10: Mood in Verbs

1. All verbs in the English language have which of the following?

Ⓐ mood
Ⓑ tense
Ⓒ voice
Ⓓ all of the above

2. What of the following is NOT a mood in verbs?

Ⓐ active
Ⓑ subjunctive
Ⓒ indicative
Ⓓ imperative

3. In which of the following instances would the subjunctive mood be necessary?

Ⓐ writing about a hypothetical situation
Ⓑ making a wish
Ⓒ making a suggestion
Ⓓ all of the above

4. What is the mood of a verb?

Ⓐ how the author feels before writing
Ⓑ what state of mind the author is in when writing
Ⓒ the author's attitude about what he is writing
Ⓓ none of the above

5. The indicative mood of a verb does what?

Ⓐ gives a command
Ⓑ states a fact
Ⓒ expresses a wish
Ⓓ states a condition

6. The imperative mood of a verb does what?

Ⓐ gives a command
Ⓑ states a fact
Ⓒ expresses a wish
Ⓓ states a condition

7. The subjunctive mood of a verb does what?

Ⓐ gives a command
Ⓑ states a fact
Ⓒ expresses a wish
Ⓓ states a condition

8. Part A
Which of the following sentences is written in the subjunctive mood?

Ⓐ It will rain tomorrow.
Ⓑ It might rain tomorrow.
Ⓒ Prepare for the rain tomorrow.
Ⓓ None of the above

Part B
Which of the following sentences is written in the imperative mood?

Ⓐ It will rain tomorrow.
Ⓑ It might rain tomorrow.
Ⓒ Prepare for the rain tomorrow.
Ⓓ None of the above

9. Which of the following sentences is written in the indicative mood?

Ⓐ It will rain tomorrow.
Ⓑ It might rain tomorrow.
Ⓒ Prepare for the rain tomorrow.
Ⓓ None of the above

Test ID	8E033
Test Name	**Active and Passive Voice**
Student Name	
Date	

1	Ⓐ Ⓑ Ⓒ Ⓓ	**6**	Ⓐ Ⓑ Ⓒ Ⓓ	**11**	Answer in the space provided below.
2	Ⓐ Ⓑ Ⓒ Ⓓ	**7**	Ⓐ Ⓑ Ⓒ Ⓓ	**12**	Answer in the space provided below.
3	Ⓐ Ⓑ Ⓒ Ⓓ	**8**	Ⓐ Ⓑ Ⓒ Ⓓ		
4	Ⓐ Ⓑ Ⓒ Ⓓ	**9**	Ⓐ Ⓑ Ⓒ Ⓓ		
5	Ⓐ Ⓑ Ⓒ Ⓓ	**10**	Ⓐ Ⓑ Ⓒ Ⓓ		

11

12

Chapter 3 → Lesson 11: Active and Passive Voice

1. What comes first in active voice?

Ⓐ subject
Ⓑ object
Ⓒ action
Ⓓ fall

2. What is passive voice?

Ⓐ When the writer uses a very nice tone of voice
Ⓑ When the writer says nice things
Ⓒ A sentence that is not a question or command
Ⓓ A sentence in which the subject is acted upon instead of doing the action

3. What is active voice?

Ⓐ When somebody talks a lot
Ⓑ A sentence with a lot of action
Ⓒ A sentence in which the subject is performing the action
Ⓓ When someone talks and performs an activity at the same time

4. Is the following sentence written in active or passive voice?

Margaret is loved by Brian.

Ⓐ active
Ⓑ passive
Ⓒ neither
Ⓓ both

5. Is the following sentence written in active or passive voice?

The stray dog was being taken care of by Matthew.

Ⓐ active
Ⓑ passive
Ⓒ neither
Ⓓ both

6. Is the following sentence written in active or passive voice?

Samantha sewed the hem of her sister's wedding dress when it ripped.

Ⓐ active
Ⓑ passive
Ⓒ neither
Ⓓ both

7. Which of the following sentences is written in active voice?

    a) One day that dress will be handed down to me by my mother.
    b) My father always changes the oil in our vehicles by himself.
    c) I made chocolate chip cookies for the birthday party.
    d) That cabinet was made by my grandfather.

Ⓐ a and b
Ⓑ b and c
Ⓒ d and c
Ⓓ a and d

8. Which of the following sentences are written in active voice?

    a) This house was built by my uncle.
    b) This wonderful dessert was baked by my mother.

Ⓐ a
Ⓑ b
Ⓒ both a and b
Ⓓ none of the above

9. Which of the following sentences is written in active voice?

    a) Everybody should eat vegetables.
    b) At the concert, one audience member will be selected to participate.
    c) Everyone should learn how to swim as early as possible.

Ⓐ a
Ⓑ b
Ⓒ c
Ⓓ all of the above
Ⓔ none of the above

10. Which of the following sentences is written in passive voice.

a) One day, that dress will be handed down to me by my mother.
b) My father always changes the oil in our vehicles by himself.
c) I made chocolate chip cookies for the birthday party.
d) My grandfather made that cabinet.

Ⓐ a
Ⓑ b
Ⓒ c
Ⓓ d

11. Identify whether the following sentence is written in the active or passive voice.

Much to her mother's dismay, Chloe colored on the dining room table.

Write your answer in the box given below.

12. Identify whether the following sentence is written in the active or passive voice.

Camille was going to make dinner for everyone before she went to bed.

Write your answer in the box given below.

Test ID	8E034
Test Name	**Context Clues**
Student Name	
Date	

1	Ⓐ Ⓑ Ⓒ Ⓓ	**6**	Ⓐ Ⓑ Ⓒ Ⓓ	**11**	Ⓐ Ⓑ Ⓒ Ⓓ
2	Ⓐ Ⓑ Ⓒ Ⓓ	**7**	Ⓐ Ⓑ Ⓒ Ⓓ	**12**	Ⓐ Ⓑ Ⓒ Ⓓ
3	Ⓐ Ⓑ Ⓒ Ⓓ	**8**	Ⓐ Ⓑ Ⓒ Ⓓ		
4	Ⓐ Ⓑ Ⓒ Ⓓ	**9**	Ⓐ Ⓑ Ⓒ Ⓓ		
5	Ⓐ Ⓑ Ⓒ Ⓓ	**10**	Ⓐ Ⓑ Ⓒ Ⓓ		

Chapter 3 → Lesson 12: Context Clues

1. The context of a word means _____.

   Ⓐ the words that surround it
   Ⓑ words that don't mean the same as they say
   Ⓒ using detail
   Ⓓ finding facts to support

2. What should you do when using context clues?

   Ⓐ Read the sentence containing the unfamiliar word, leaving that word out.
   Ⓑ Look closely at the words around the unfamiliar word to help guess its meaning.
   Ⓒ Substitute a possible meaning for the word and read the sentence to see if it makes sense.
   Ⓓ all of the above

3. Brian appeared infallible on the basketball court because he never missed a shot.

What is the best meaning of infallible?

   Ⓐ incapable of making an error
   Ⓑ imperfect
   Ⓒ faulty
   Ⓓ unsure of what he's doing

4. After the police broke up a skirmish between opposing groups, everyone went their separate ways.

What is the best meaning of skirmish?

   Ⓐ peace protest
   Ⓑ fight
   Ⓒ theft
   Ⓓ agreement

5. What is the best meaning of excruciating?

   Ⓐ bearable
   Ⓑ extremely pleasant
   Ⓒ unbearable
   Ⓓ soon went away

LumosLearning.com

6. Michael's overt flirting with Michelle during lunch drew the attention of Larry, her boyfriend.

   What is the best meaning of overt?

   Ⓐ concealed
   Ⓑ hidden
   Ⓒ obvious
   Ⓓ secret

7. Vanity got the best of Sarah as she ran into the wall while checking her hair in the mirror at the end of the hallway.

   What is the best meaning of vanity?

   Ⓐ modestly
   Ⓑ pride in one's qualities
   Ⓒ lack of real value
   Ⓓ tried things in vain

8. Becca's rude and pithy response to her teacher only took a second, but it landed her a week in after school detention.

   What is the best meaning of pithy?

   Ⓐ brief
   Ⓑ long winded
   Ⓒ sweet
   Ⓓ impolite

9. His emotions were difficult to articulate, but Fredrick knew it was now or never. He had to tell Francie how much he loved her before she got on the bus and left him and his heart forever.

   What is the best meaning for the word articulate?

   Ⓐ unclear
   Ⓑ clearly spoken
   Ⓒ hidden
   Ⓓ move in segments

10. **The pungent odor of my mom's shower cleaning fluid burned my nostrils and made it hard for me to breathe.**
   What is the best meaning of pungent?

   Ⓐ pleasant
   Ⓑ bland
   Ⓒ sharp or acidy
   Ⓓ odorless

Bailey had a sense of foreboding as she walked into the classroom. She noticed that all the bulletin boards were covered up and the privacy folders were lying on the desks. Had she forgotten a test?

11. **What is the best definition of foreboding?**

   Ⓐ good fortune
   Ⓑ bad feeling
   Ⓒ fortune
   Ⓓ anticipation

Bruce proved his incredible stamina as he jumped rope for twenty minutes without a break.

12. **Which is the best definition of stamina?**

   Ⓐ laziness
   Ⓑ strength, vigor
   Ⓒ weakness
   Ⓓ fatigue

Test ID	8E035
Test Name	**Multiple Meaning Words**
Student Name	
Date	

1	(A) (B) (C) (D)	6	(A) (B) (C) (D)	11	(A) (B) (C) (D) (E) (F)	
2	(A) (B) (C) (D)	7	(A) (B) (C) (D)			
3	(A) (B) (C) (D)	8	(A) (B) (C) (D)			
4	(A) (B)	9	(A) (B) (C) (D)			
5	(A) (B) (C) (D)	10	(A) (B) (C) (D)			

Chapter 3 → Lesson 13: Multiple Meaning Words

1. What is a homonym?

Ⓐ words that sound the same but have different meanings and spellings.
Ⓑ words that sound the same and have the same spelling but different meaning.
Ⓒ words that do not sound the same or have the same spelling or meaning.
Ⓓ words that neither sound or look alike.

2. What is the correct definition of a homophone?

Ⓐ words that sound and look alike.
Ⓑ words that sound alike but are spelled differently.
Ⓒ words that sound different but mean the same thing.
Ⓓ none of the above.

3. Which meaning of the word "address" is used in the following sentence?

One should always address the president as, "Mr. President".

Ⓐ a formal communication
Ⓑ a place where a person or organization can be contacted
Ⓒ to direct a speech
Ⓓ the place you live

4. Which of the homophones, "complement" and "compliment," will correctly fit into the following sentence?

I like to wear my blue, flowered dress. Whenever I wear it I receive a lot of _____ (s).

Ⓐ compliment
Ⓑ complement

5. Which meaning of the word "strike" is used in the following sentence?

If the two sides cannot come to an agreement, there will be a strike.

Ⓐ to aim and deliver a blow
Ⓑ to lower a flag, as in surrender
Ⓒ to knock all the pins down in bowling
Ⓓ to stop work in an attempt to force an employer to comply with demands

6. Choose the word that is a synonym for the underlined word in the following sentence.

Amanda has not been feeling well lately. She went to visit her doctor today to <u>determine</u> why she has been under the weather.

Ⓐ settle
Ⓑ decline
Ⓒ abstain
Ⓓ study

7. What is the correct definition of the word "suit" as it is used in the sentence below?

When I decided not to go to the prom, my girlfriend said, "Suit yourself. I'll find someone else to dance with."

Ⓐ formal attire
Ⓑ legal action
Ⓒ benefit
Ⓓ request

8. What is the correct definition of the word "band" as it is used in the sentence below?

Let's band together to stamp out hunger!

Ⓐ encircle
Ⓑ a group of people with the same interest
Ⓒ to come together
Ⓓ a musical group

9. What is the correct definition of the word "fair" as it is used in the sentence below?

I couldn't wait for the fair to come to town. Nothing beats a funnel cake from the fair!

Ⓐ impartial
Ⓑ a carnival
Ⓒ equal
Ⓓ a charge for transportation

10. What are the two possible definitions for the word stalk?

(A) a part of a plant
(B) a part of a human
(C) to follow someone
(D) to be the leader

11. Which are the synonyms of graduation. More than one answer may be correct. Select all the correct ones.

(A) completion
(B) confidence
(C) realize
(D) concentration
(E) culmination
(F) close

1	Ⓐ Ⓑ Ⓒ Ⓓ	6	Ⓐ Ⓑ Ⓒ Ⓓ	11	Answer in the space provided below.
2	Ⓐ Ⓑ Ⓒ Ⓓ	7	Ⓐ Ⓑ Ⓒ Ⓓ	12	Ⓐ Ⓑ Ⓒ Ⓓ
3	Ⓐ Ⓑ Ⓒ Ⓓ	8	Ⓐ Ⓑ Ⓒ Ⓓ		
4	Ⓐ Ⓑ Ⓒ Ⓓ	9	Ⓐ Ⓑ Ⓒ Ⓓ		
5	Ⓐ Ⓑ Ⓒ Ⓓ	10	Ⓐ Ⓑ Ⓒ Ⓓ		

11

	full of care	someone who applies for something	a person who specializes in studying the history of the earth, including rocks
The suffix "ist" means a skilled person in. a geologist is	◯	◯	◯
The suffix "ful" means full of. Therefore the word "careful" means:	◯	◯	◯
The suffix "ant" means a person who. Applicant means	◯	◯	◯

Chapter 3 → Lesson 14: Roots, Affixes, and Syllables

1. Where does the prefix go in a word?

- Ⓐ at the end
- Ⓑ at the beginning
- Ⓒ in the middle
- Ⓓ none of the above

2. Where does a suffix go in a word?

- Ⓐ at the end
- Ⓑ at the beginning
- Ⓒ in the middle
- Ⓓ none of the above

3. What is an affix?

- Ⓐ a repair for something
- Ⓑ a prefix or suffix attached to a root to form a new word
- Ⓒ a sound made by blends of letters
- Ⓓ the phonetic understanding of words

4. What is the best definition of a "root" of a word?

- Ⓐ the beginning of a word
- Ⓑ the end of a word
- Ⓒ the base of a word
- Ⓓ the middle of the word

5. What is a syllable?

- Ⓐ the sound of a vowel when pronouncing a word
- Ⓑ what a teacher gives students that outlines what will be studied in class
- Ⓒ the sound of a consonant when pronouncing a word
- Ⓓ a prefix or suffix attached to a root to form a new word

6. An omnivore is an animal that eats both plants and meat. What does the prefix omni mean?

- Ⓐ everywhere or everything
- Ⓑ animal
- Ⓒ to eat
- Ⓓ starvation

7. Identify the affixes in the following words?

mislead, unrestricted, reiterate

Ⓐ mis, un, re
Ⓑ lead, ed, ate
Ⓒ lead, stricted, rate
Ⓓ lead, restricted, iterate

8. The root word, cede means, "to go". With this knowledge, determine the meaning of the word, "precede".

Ⓐ to go after
Ⓑ to go away
Ⓒ to go before
Ⓓ to go never

9. Dynamic means physical force or energy. What does the root word "dyna" mean?

Ⓐ to be weak
Ⓑ power
Ⓒ to be little
Ⓓ to be tired

10. The prefix "un" means not. What does "unable" mean?

Ⓐ ready
Ⓑ not able
Ⓒ unclear
Ⓓ not unable

11. Match the word to its meaning based on the suffix

	full of care	someone who applies for something	a person who specializes in studying the history of the earth, including rocks
The suffix "ist" means a skilled person in. a geologist is			
The suffix "ful" means full of. Therefore the word "careful" means:			
The suffix "ant" means a person who. Applicant means			

12. The suffix "er" means a person who does an action. What does "announcer" mean?

Ⓐ someone who announces
Ⓑ someone who works on automobiles
Ⓒ someone who works for a news station
Ⓓ all of the above

Test ID	8E037
Test Name	**Reference Materials**
Student Name	
Date	

1	(A) (B) (C) (D) (E)	5 A	(A) (B) (C) (D)
2 A	(A) (B) (C) (D)	5 B	(A) (B) (C) (D)
2 B	(A) (B) (C) (D) (E)	6	(A) (B) (C)
3	(A) (B) (C) (D)	7	(A) (B) (C) (D)
4	(A) (B) (C) (D)	8	(A) (B) (C) (D)

Chapter 3 → Lesson 15: Reference Materials

1. **Which of the following are acceptable reference materials to use for a research assignment?**

   Ⓐ questionnaires
   Ⓑ experiments
   Ⓒ field studies
   Ⓓ scholarly articles
   Ⓔ all of the above

2. **Part A**
   What are primary sources?

   Ⓐ materials that come directly from the source
   Ⓑ materials that have been copied from the source
   Ⓒ materials that are found only in encyclopedias
   Ⓓ materials that are over 100 years old

   Part B
   Which of the following are examples of secondary sources?

   Ⓐ biographies
   Ⓑ encyclopedias
   Ⓒ textbooks
   Ⓓ documentaries
   Ⓔ all of the above

3. **How can you determine whether a source is reliable?**

   Ⓐ If you obtained your information from the Internet, it is always reliable.
   Ⓑ You should consider who wrote the source and why.
   Ⓒ If you obtained your information from an actual article, it will be reliable.
   Ⓓ answer choices B & C

4. **Why must you be very careful about obtaining information from websites?**

   Ⓐ It can be difficult to find reputable sources.
   Ⓑ Some sites can be edited by anyone.
   Ⓒ It is too easy to find what may look like good information but sources are often unverifiable.
   Ⓓ All of the above

5. **Part A**
   What are the benefits of using primary sources?

   Ⓐ They are first-hand accounts from those who witnessed or experienced the event being researched.
   Ⓑ They offer a limited perspective.
   Ⓒ They haven't been very well researched.
   Ⓓ They are reposted hundreds of times.

   Part B
   What are the benefits of using secondary sources?

   Ⓐ They have been analyzed and interpreted.
   Ⓑ They have not often used a variety of primary sources to come to their conclusions.
   Ⓒ They are straight from the source.
   Ⓓ They have been reposted hundreds of times.

6. **What do the following items have in common?**

   diary
   journal
   letter
   official letters

   Ⓐ They are secondary sources.
   Ⓑ They are primary sources.
   Ⓒ They are neither primary nor secondary sources.

7. **What do the following items have in common?**

   books
   journal articles
   textbooks
   reference sources

   Ⓐ They are primary sources.
   Ⓑ They are secondary sources.
   Ⓒ Some are secondary sources.
   Ⓓ None of the above

8. **If you were researching Anne Frank, which of the following would be your choice for a primary source?**

Ⓐ your teacher
Ⓑ an encyclopedia
Ⓒ a website about Anne Frank
Ⓓ Anne Frank's diary

Test ID	8E038
Test Name	**Using Context to Verify Meaning**
Student Name	
Date	

1	Ⓐ Ⓑ Ⓒ Ⓓ	6	Ⓐ Ⓑ Ⓒ Ⓓ
2	Ⓐ Ⓑ Ⓒ Ⓓ	7	Ⓐ Ⓑ Ⓒ Ⓓ
3	Ⓐ Ⓑ Ⓒ Ⓓ	8 A	Ⓐ Ⓑ Ⓒ Ⓓ
4	Ⓐ Ⓑ Ⓒ Ⓓ	8 B	Ⓐ Ⓑ Ⓒ Ⓓ
5	Ⓐ Ⓑ Ⓒ Ⓓ	9	Ⓐ Ⓑ Ⓒ Ⓓ

Chapter 3 → Lesson 16: Using Context to Verify Meaning

Question 1-9 are based on the passage below

Marathon

Training for a marathon takes hard work and **perseverance**. It is not something you can do on the **spur** of the moment. Preparing for a marathon takes months, particularly if you have never run a marathon before. The official distance of a full marathon is 26.2 miles. In 2005, the average time to complete a marathon in the United States was 4 hours 32 minutes 8 seconds for men and 5 hours 6 minutes 8 seconds for women.

Most people who run marathons are not trying to win. Many runners try to beat their own best time. Some compare their time to other runners in the same gender and age group. Some people set time-oriented goals, such as finishing under four hours, while others try to complete the race without slowing to a walk. Many beginners simply hope to finish the marathon.

Trainers recommend that beginners maintain a **consistent** running schedule for six weeks prior to even starting a marathon training program. The purpose of this is to allow the body to adapt to the **various** physical demands of long-distance running. First-time marathon runners should train by running four days a week for at least four months, increasing distance by no more than ten percent weekly. As race day approaches, runners should **taper** their runs, reducing the strain on their bodies and resting before the marathon. It is important not to over**exert** yourself during training because that can lead to a lot of injuries. Most common injuries are spraining of the knees and ankles. These sprains can **hinder** the training.

Before the race, it is important to stretch in order to keep muscles **limber**. Staying hydrated is also important, but there is a danger in drinking too much water. If a runner drinks too much water, they may experience a dangerous condition called **hyponatremia**, a drop of sodium levels in the blood. During the race, trainers recommend maintaining a steady pace. It is normal to feel sore after a marathon. Light exercise will help sore muscles heal faster.

Some people run marathons in pairs or groups. Training for and running a marathon with another person or group of people can make the experience more enjoyable and more rewarding. A running partner might be just the motivation you need to show up for an early morning run instead of rolling over to hit the snooze button. And, when you cross the finish line together, you can share the satisfaction of reaching your common goal.

Usually, thousands of people sign up and run a marathon. Most people finish the race. The thrill of running a marathon for the first time is unbelievable. The training sessions are harder if you have never run before. But it is unbelievable what ones' body can do when one puts his/her mind to it. Having a good coach to support you makes all the difference in training for a marathon.

The daily runs are very important. Strength training and core training are also very important.

Using context clues in the story, determine the meaning of the *bold* words.

1. perseverance

- Ⓐ determination
- Ⓑ routine
- Ⓒ flexibility
- Ⓓ practice

2. spur

- Ⓐ after long planning
- Ⓑ without planning
- Ⓒ with much discussion
- Ⓓ with significant thought

3. consistent

- Ⓐ varying
- Ⓑ changing
- Ⓒ regular
- Ⓓ dynamic

4. various

- Ⓐ many
- Ⓑ few
- Ⓒ hard
- Ⓓ simple

5. taper

- Ⓐ add more
- Ⓑ pick and choose
- Ⓒ scale back
- Ⓓ candle

6. exert

- Ⓐ sleep
- Ⓑ utilize
- Ⓒ rest
- Ⓓ run

7. hinder

Ⓐ delay
Ⓑ speed up
Ⓒ help
Ⓓ assist

8. Part A
limber

Ⓐ tone
Ⓑ tight
Ⓒ loose
Ⓓ wavy

8. Part B

hyponatremia

Ⓐ a drop of sodium levels in the blood
Ⓑ dehydration
Ⓒ a pulled muscle
Ⓓ easily able to swim

9. If you cannot determine a word's meaning in context, where can you look? From the 4 choices given below, select the correct answer and enter it in the box given below.

Ⓐ thesaurus
Ⓑ dictionary
Ⓒ encyclopedia
Ⓓ journal

Test ID	8E039
Test Name	Interpreting Figures of Speech
Student Name	
Date	

1	(A) (B) (C) (D)	6	(A) (B) (C) (D)	11	Answer in the space provided below.
2	(A) (B) (C) (D)	7	(A) (B) (C) (D)	12	Answer in the space provided below.
3	(A) (B) (C) (D)	8	(A) (B) (C) (D)	13	Answer in the space provided below.
4	(A) (B) (C) (D)	9	(A) (B) (C) (D)		
5	(A) (B) (C) (D)	10	(A) (B) (C) (D)		

11

12

13

Chapter 3 → Lesson 17: Interpreting Figures of Speech

1. How is a metaphor different than a simile?

- Ⓐ A metaphor is the same as a simile.
- Ⓑ A metaphor does not use like or as in the comparison of two unlike things.
- Ⓒ A metaphor is not at all similar to a simile.
- Ⓓ A metaphor uses like or as in the comparison of two unlike things.

2. What two figures of speech listed below have to do with word sounds?

- Ⓐ metaphor and simile
- Ⓑ personification and idiom
- Ⓒ alliteration and onomatopoeia
- Ⓓ noun and verb

3. Which of the following is a metaphor?

- Ⓐ It is as hot as the surface of the sun out there.
- Ⓑ She sold seashells by the seashore.
- Ⓒ I stayed up too late last night studying and now my mind is foggy.
- Ⓓ She plopped on the sofa after babysitting nine hours.

4. What does the idiom "burning the candle at both ends" mean?

- Ⓐ You are wasting wax.
- Ⓑ You are doing too much.
- Ⓒ You are preparing for an emergency.
- Ⓓ You have a great need for a lot of light.

5. What is the meaning of the following simile?

Her eyes are like fiery diamonds.

- Ⓐ sparkly and bright
- Ⓑ hard and hot
- Ⓒ warm and light
- Ⓓ expensive and desirable

6. Today, my brother and I went to the batting cages. I was in awe of him as I watched him hit ball after ball; he was a machine.

Why is the brother being compared to a machine?

Ⓐ He seemed to be under the control of a robot.
Ⓑ He hit every ball with accuracy and efficiency.
Ⓒ He was rigid and metal-like.
Ⓓ He didn't show much emotion as he hit the balls.

7. **What is the meaning of the following metaphor?**

He has the heart of a lion.

Ⓐ The people on the street.
Ⓑ He is hairy.
Ⓒ He has a large heart.
Ⓓ He is courageous.

8. **What figure of speech is used in the following sentence?**

The leaves of the tree danced in the breeze.

Ⓐ personification
Ⓑ metaphor
Ⓒ simile
Ⓓ idiom

9. **Donna's brother said, "You're selling yourself short." What does she mean by this?**

Ⓐ you need to grow a little taller
Ⓑ you are not giving yourself enough credit
Ⓒ you are a little short
Ⓓ you do not need to worry about being tall

10. **What figure of speech is used in the following sentence?**

I saw the coolest concert last night.

Ⓐ personification
Ⓑ alliteration
Ⓒ metaphor
Ⓓ simile

11. What figure of speech is used in the following sentence:

Sarah was like a toddler hungry for food; I was ready to get out of the car with her.

Write your answer in the box given below.

12. What figure of speech is used in the sentence below:

I heard the pop of the kernels in the microwave and knew my snack was almost ready.

Write your answer in the box given below.

13. What does the idiom "a piece of cake" mean? Write your answer in the box given below.

The teacher told us the test would be a piece of cake, but I disagree.

Test ID	8E040
Test Name	**Relationships Between Words**
Student Name	
Date	

1	(A) (B) (C) (D)	6	(A) (B) (C) (D)	11	Answer in the space provided below.
2	(A) (B) (C) (D)	7	(A) (B) (C) (D)	12	Answer in the space provided below.
3	(A) (B) (C) (D)	8	(A) (B) (C) (D)	13	Answer in the space provided below.
4	(A) (B) (C) (D)	9	(A) (B) (C) (D)		
5	(A) (B) (C) (D)	10	(A) (B) (C) (D)		

11

12

13

Chapter 3 → Lesson 18: Relationships Between Words

1. What is an analogy?

Ⓐ words that mean the opposite
Ⓑ a comparison of two words
Ⓒ a short story
Ⓓ the study of ants

2. Select the best choice to explain the relationship of the words in the following analogy.

branch is to tree as fingers are to hand

Ⓐ antonyms
Ⓑ synonyms
Ⓒ part to whole
Ⓓ whole to part

3. Select the best choice to finish the following analogy.

repel is to attract as _____ is to lead

Ⓐ follow
Ⓑ guide
Ⓒ direct
Ⓓ head

4. Select the best choice to finish the following analogy.

I is to mine as they is to _____

Ⓐ there's
Ⓑ theirs
Ⓒ they'res
Ⓓ theirses

5. Select the best choice to finish the following analogy.

ostracism is to acceptance as _____ is to charitable

Ⓐ deliberate
Ⓑ rejection
Ⓒ greedy
Ⓓ giving

6. Study the analogy below to determine the relationship between the words that are presented.

won is to one as rode is to road

Ⓐ   homonyms
Ⓑ   synonyms
Ⓒ   homophones
Ⓓ   homographs

7. Study the analogy below to determine the relationship between the words that are presented.

woman is to women as mouse is to mice

Ⓐ   present tense to past tense
Ⓑ   singular to plural
Ⓒ   plural to singular
Ⓓ   antonyms

8. Finish the following analogy.

tiny is to small as enormous is to

Ⓐ   minute
Ⓑ   monstrous
Ⓒ   large
Ⓓ   petite

9. Complete the following analogy.

television is to view as _____ is to listen

Ⓐ   radio
Ⓑ   movie
Ⓒ   computer
Ⓓ   people

10. Finish the following analogy.

woman is to girl as man is to _____

Ⓐ   son
Ⓑ   boy
Ⓒ   father
Ⓓ   dad

11. Match the word to its definition.

Analogy —

Antonyms —

Synonyms —

words that mean the same thing
words with opposite meanings
a comparison of two words

12. Match the word sets to its correct category.

Synonyms —

Antonyms —

Analogy —

highlight - emphasize
Grape:Rasin::Plum:Prune
detached - interested

13. Words that express extreme exaggeration are called as _____

Identify the figure of speech defined by above sentence.

Test ID	8E041
Test Name	**Denotations and Connotations**
Student Name	
Date	

1 A	(A) (B) (C) (D)	5	(A) (B) (C) (D)	10	Answer in the space provided below.
1 B	(A) (B) (C) (D)	6	(A) (B) (C)	11	Answer in the space provided below.
2	(A) (B) (C)	7	(A) (B) (C) (D)		
3	(A) (B) (C) (D)	8	(A) (B) (C) (D)		
4	(A) (B) (C)	9	(A) (B) (C) (D)		

10

×

+

11

×

+

Chapter 3 → Lesson 19: Denotations and Connotations

1. Part A
What is the definition of <u>denotation</u>?

Ⓐ   the feelings or ideas a word suggests
Ⓑ   the actual dictionary definition of a word
Ⓒ   a word that is a symbol of the opposite word
Ⓓ   words that have the same meanings

Part B
What is the definition of <u>connotation</u>?

Ⓐ   the feelings or ideas a word suggests
Ⓑ   the actual dictionary definition of a word
Ⓒ   a word that is a symbol of the opposite word
Ⓓ   a word that means the same thing

2. The denotation of a word is the literal dictionary definition. The connotation of a word is the idea or feeling associated with the word.

Is the underlined word used denotatively or connotatively?

That girl is <u>immature</u> and impossible to be around because she is always goofing around and is a huge disruption in class.

Ⓐ   denotatively
Ⓑ   connotatively
Ⓒ   both

3. Which of the following words has the most positive connotation?

dwelling, house, home, residence

Ⓐ   dwelling
Ⓑ   house
Ⓒ   home
Ⓓ   residence

4. Which of the following words has the most negative connotation?

cheap, frugal, thrifty

Ⓐ   cheap
Ⓑ   frugal
Ⓒ   thrifty

5. Which of the following has the most positive connotation?

Ⓐ plain
Ⓑ dull
Ⓒ ugly
Ⓓ unattractive

6. Which word has the most neutral connotation?

assertive, pushy, aggressive

Ⓐ assertive
Ⓑ pushy
Ⓒ aggressive

7. What is a negative connotation for funny?

Ⓐ absurd
Ⓑ uncommon
Ⓒ comical
Ⓓ amusing

8. What would a negative connotation for the word "quick" be?

Ⓐ prompt
Ⓑ rapid
Ⓒ hasty
Ⓓ responsive

9. What is a neutral connotation for small?

Ⓐ short
Ⓑ paltry
Ⓒ insignificant
Ⓓ trivial

10. My mom screamed when she realized she won first place in the pie baking contest.

Does the word "screamed" in the above sentence have a positive, negative, or neutral connotation?

11. My mom screamed as she fell off the ladder into the bushes.

Does the word "screamed" in the above sentence have a positive, negative, or neutral connotation?

Test ID	8E042
Test Name	**Domain Specific Words**
Student Name	
Date	

1	Ⓐ Ⓑ Ⓒ Ⓓ	**6**	Ⓐ Ⓑ Ⓒ Ⓓ
2	Ⓐ Ⓑ Ⓒ Ⓓ	**7**	Ⓐ Ⓑ Ⓒ Ⓓ
3	Ⓐ Ⓑ Ⓒ Ⓓ	**8**	Answer in the space provided below.
4	Ⓐ Ⓑ Ⓒ Ⓓ	**9**	Answer in the space provided below.
5	Ⓐ Ⓑ Ⓒ Ⓓ	**10**	Answer in the space provided below.

8

9

10

Chapter 3 → Lesson 20: Domain Specific Words

1. What is jargon?

Ⓐ words that are silly
Ⓑ words that are specific to an area a study
Ⓒ words that are slang
Ⓓ words that describe nouns

2. Given the task to write an essay about literature, what would be a good domain specific vocabulary word to use?

Ⓐ plot
Ⓑ characterization
Ⓒ dialogue
Ⓓ all of the above

3. Read the sentence below; identify a domain specific vocabulary word in it.

After reading the novel, it is clear that the author's use of setting is meant a symbol for bravery.

Ⓐ symbol
Ⓑ bravery
Ⓒ use
Ⓓ author's

4. Which of the following words would best fit in the following sentence?

Samuel felt _____ by his teachers consistent nagging about his grades. He knew he needed to bring them up, and her constant reminders increased his anxiety.

Ⓐ angry
Ⓑ annoyed
Ⓒ frustrated
Ⓓ mad

5. What word in the following sentence is a domain specific vocabulary word?

An animal's predatory instincts are what helps it survive when it needs food or protection.

Ⓐ instinct
Ⓑ animal
Ⓒ food
Ⓓ protection

6. What word in the following sentence is a domain specific vocabulary word?

The slope of the line is calculated using slope intercept form. It is important to understand this formula if you want to be a successful math student.

- Ⓐ student
- Ⓑ successful
- Ⓒ calculated
- Ⓓ important

7. What word in the following sentence is a domain specific vocabulary word?

The economy is governed by supply and demand. The market is what drives the economy and the economy is what capitalism is based upon.

- Ⓐ market
- Ⓑ economy
- Ⓒ capitalism
- Ⓓ all of the above

8. What words in the following sentences is a domain specific vocabulary words?

The poem can be interpreted in many ways. Readers can begin their interpretation by looking at a poem's meter, and then by closely examining its rhyme scheme and its rhythm. The overall interpretation should include the many nuances of the poem.

9. What word in the following sentence is a domain specific vocabulary word?

Look closely to see that the plugs and plug wires are all in good shape. Do this simple check before taking your car to the mechanic and it might save you a few bucks. Keep your money in your pocket if you can.

10. What word in the following sentence is a domain specific vocabulary word?

Check the motherboard first. If the motherboard is fried, you might as well just go to the store and get a new computer. There is no sense in spending that much time and energy to fix your machine if the brain of it is broken.

End of Language

Test Mastery tedBook by Lumos Learning - 8th Grade English Language Arts State (ELA) Test Prep Workbook | Two Online Grade 8 ELA Practice Tests & Learning Resources: Covers Reading: Literature, Reading: Informational Text, and Language (Ages 13-14)

Contributing Author - Erin Schollaert
Contributing Author - Nina Anderson
Contributing Author - George Smith
Executive Producer - Mukunda Krishnaswamy
Program Director - Anirudh Agarwal
Designer and Illustrator - Sowmya R.

ISBN 13:978-1959697602

Printed in the United States of America

CONTACT INFORMATION

LUMOS INFORMATION SERVICES, LLC

 PO Box 1575, Piscataway, NJ 08855-1575
 www.LumosLearning.com

 Email: support@lumoslearning.com
 Tel: (732) 384-0146
 Fax: (866) 283-6471

Step Up Your Skills

How to Use the Answer Booklet

1. Use the **Table of Contents** to find the lesson you wish to practice.

2. Use a **2B pencil** to answer the questions.
   Marking Instruction: Completely fill in the appropriate bubble.

   Correct ●   Incorrect ⊗ ⊘ ⊙ ⊙

3. For open-ended questions, write your answer in the boxes provided on the answer sheet.

4. After completing a lesson, take a clear picture of the answer sheet and upload it using the **SCAN ANSWER SHEET** option provided in the student account. Alternatively, your teacher may also scan and upload the answer sheet.

5. Once uploaded, follow the instructions to get the results. Open-ended questions will be graded by your teacher.

Made in the USA
Las Vegas, NV
14 February 2024

85800145R00125

Sew Fast - Sew Easy

SEW CUSHIONS

DOROTHEA HALL

WARD LOCK

First published in the UK 1995
by Ward Lock
Wellington House
125 Strand
LONDON
WC2R 0BB

A Cassell Imprint

Designed and produced by
Tucker Slingsby Ltd
3G London House
66–68 Upper Richmond Road
London SW15 2RP

A British Library Cataloguing in Publication Data block for this book may be obtained from
the British Library

ISBN 0 7063 7379 0

Printed and bound in Singapore

CONTENTS

Before You Begin

Cushion Style

Cushions are quick and inexpensive to make and have many uses, both practical and decorative. The cushions shown in the following pages illustrate the amazing variety of shapes, fabrics and finishing touches that you can choose between. There is something here to suit every style of interior – from country cottage to high-rise apartment.

Cushion co-ordination

If you are lucky enough to have the opportunity to create a whole new look for a room, by buying furniture, carpets and curtains all at the same time, then a careful choice of contrasting and matching cushion covers will provide the perfect finishing touch to your interior design.

Making cushions in the same fabric as your curtains is one of the simplest ways to achieve a co-ordinated look in a room, but there are many other ways of using cushions to complement your interior design. Cushions can be finished with piping or frills that pick up and echo other colours in the room. A wide range of cords and braids is now available and these can also be used to complement or contrast with other elements in your room design.

Making new cushions is also a quick and inexpensive way of creating

a co-ordinated look when you have inherited a mixture of colours and styles that need pulling together. Look for fabrics that pick up and reflect colours and patterns from your curtains, carpet and furniture, and use them to make a selection of cushions. Distribute these cushions generously around the room on sofas and chairs. This will create a feeling of unity as well as of comfort.

Cushion groups

A group of co-ordinated cushions always looks effective whether introduced into an existing setting or specially created for a new interior. A sofa, for example, may be covered in a floral chintz and scattered with plain cushions covered in plain-textured damasks, geometric checks and stripes – all in colours picked up from the floral chintz.

Here, floral prints are cleverly mixed with plain-textured velvet, woven tartans and geometric designs to create a charming collection of co-ordinating cushions. The complexity of the fabric designs is offset by the plain shape of the cushions, which have simple piped edges.

For a simpler but equally effective group of matching cushions, choose two fabrics and mix and match them between the cover and a contrasting frill or piping. So, for example, you can sew a mixture of red cushions with blue piping and blue cushions with red piping.

An existing group of cushions can be refreshed with new cord around the edge, tassels sewn on and a couple of new cushions added to tone with the new trimmings.

Inspired by the opulence of classical furniture and fabrics – rich red and gold damasks – this cushion collection makes a real impact. The rectangular cushions and bolster are corded, bordered and fringed. Despite the formality of the fabrics, the mixture of sizes creates a feeling of comfort.

Cushion fun

Just as you can create special summer and winter cushions, you can make celebration cushions for Christmas, Eastertime and other occasions. In this way, you can expand your collection with every season.

Specially printed Christmas fabrics covered with holly sprigs and tiny stars, for example, are available, as are a range of colourful green, red and gold fabrics, which can be used in appliqué and patchwork techniques. For Easter, choose yellow, white or pale green fabrics and appliqué with eggs, rabbits or flowers.

Cushion gifts

An individually made cushion always makes a thoughtful and unusual gift. Sew a fun cushion tied around like a present with a huge bow or, following the simple appliqué or quilting techniques described in this book, you can sew an appropriate motif or name to decorate a cushion for a birthday or anniversary gift. Try to choose fabric to match the recipient's decor.

Fill a simple cushion shape with pot pourri or put a drop of sweet-smelling essential oil on the cushion pad to make a scented gift.

For a St Valentine's present, make a heart-shaped cushion adding a lace, ribbon or fabric frill around the edge to soften the effect.

Cushion adaptability

As well as helping to pull together the colours and fabrics in a room, cushions in bright, sunny colours can be used to lift a drab or badly lit room, while cushions in contrasting colours can highlight a focal point.

Currently, there is a revival of the Edwardian practice of having summer- and winter-weight furnishings. With springtime, the heavy brocades and chenille furnishings were cleaned and stored away to be replaced with cotton prints and lace. Changing cushion covers with the seasons provides an opportunity for cleaning and repairs and enables you to choose cool, fresh fabrics for summer and warmer, heavier fabrics for winter.

You may not want to create two sets of cushion covers to change with the seasons, but making the front and back of your covers in different fabrics gives you a chance to create a different look at the turn of a cushion.

Another way to achieve a new look in a room, with only the cost of making a small selection of cushions, is to add some vibrantly coloured round, half-circle or triangular cushions alongside existing square cushions. This will brighten up a dull corner and create a talking point.

Cool blue and white bring the outdoors indoors with these large, self-bordered cushions. The bold fabric has been cleverly cut to showcase the design. These cushions form part of a totally co-ordinated colour scheme. Note the matching bolster under the two large cushions.

Blue and cream checks bring a cool freshness to this summertime decorative scheme. Reflecting the plain and checked patterns of the sofa fabric, these self-bordered and buttoned cushions combine perfectly thanks to the use of complementary colour and pattern.

Fabrics

Cushion covers can be made from any woven fabric: light-weight cottons and silks are perfect for a bedroom but, where cushions are likely to be subjected to wear and tear, furnishing-weight fabrics are recommended. Many of these fabrics are treated to resist stains, creases and fading, making them more durable and, therefore, a more practical choice.

Furnishing fabrics are made in several widths: the most widely available is 122cm (48in) but specialist suppliers will also keep 137cm (54in) and 152cm (60in). The choice of fabric colours and textures is enormous, ranging from plain dyed and printed cottons, linens, denims, velvets, silks and satins to woven gingham, ticking, brocade and damask.

If you are planning new soft furnishings, be sure to take cushions into account and buy enough fabric to make matching cushion covers. If your decor suits a mixture of patterns and textures, look out for cushion-sized remnants in sales and on market stalls. A small piece of an expensive fabric may be on sale far below its usual price. Look in antique shops for badly torn quilts or clothes from which you can salvage enough fabric to make a cushion.

Estimating fabric amounts

The easiest way to work out the amount of fabric required for a cushion is to measure a pad of the size and shape you want, adding seam allowances all round. Unless the closure is to be slipstitched, you will also need to allow extra fabric for an overlapping closure, ties or inserting a zip. And if you want to add a frill or covered piping, then you will again need extra fabric. How to calculate fabric amounts exactly is explained on the relevant pages. Covers for soft, loose pads need to be made to give a snug fit or else you will have a rather flat cushion. Covers for firm pads, such as those used in bolsters, need to be made exactly to size.

Boldly patterned fabric can be used to make very striking cushions.

Handwash or dryclean?

Most department-store salespeople will be able to tell you the correct cleaning method for a particular fabric. As a general rule, plain-dyed and printed cottons can be carefully hand-laundered and steam pressed on the wrong side. If you press fabric on the right side, use a pressing cloth to avoid putting a sheen on the fabric. However, those cottons that have been given special finishes, such as glazing and fire-retardant sprays, should be professionally drycleaned. Delicate or luxury fabrics, such as woven brocades, velvets and silks, should also be drycleaned.

Pre-shrinking

Many hand-washable fabrics are already pre-shrunk when sold, and this will be indicated on the label. If you are not sure whether a washable fabric is pre-shrunk, cut out two 8cm (3in) squares from the fabric. Wash and iron one square and compare it with the other. If the washed square has shrunk, soak the main fabric in warm water for half an hour, having clipped the selvedges every 10cm (4in). Squeeze out the water and dry on a line. Iron when nearly dry. Fabrics to be drycleaned should be steam pressed on the wrong side.

Pads and fillings

Cushions can be made in any shape and size. If you want a conventional shape, such as a square, rectangle or round cushion, you will usually be able to buy a ready-made pad. For more unusual shapes, you may have to make the pad.

Where a relatively simple shape is required, it is sometimes possible to re-stitch a purchased pad into the shape you want. Use the instructions for making a triangular pad on page 21 as a guide. To make a pad from scratch, first make a paper pattern in the shape and size you want. Use this pattern to cut out the fabric for the pad, adding seam allowances. Use a firmly woven fabric for the pad so that the main cover can be removed for cleaning. Make up the pad following the instructions for the simple cushion shapes.

Cushion pads can be filled with feathers, or with synthetic or kapok stuffing. If you choose feathers it is best to use a wax-coated casing fabric to stop the feathers coming through.

Basic Sewing Equipment

You will need:

* Pins: longer 3cm (1¼in) pins are easier to handle on heavier fabrics.
* Sewing needles in mixed sizes.
* Thimble for hand sewing, especially through bulky seams.
* Thread:
  for tacking, use a softly twisted cotton;
  for sewing furnishing fabrics choose heavy-duty furnishing threads (cotton, cotton/polyester, or polyester) to suit the particular type of fabric being used.
* Tape measure: buy a sturdy tape measure, which will not stretch.
* Scissors: ideally, you should have three pairs:
  dressmaker's shears for cutting out fabric;
  embroidery scissors for snipping into seams and neatening threads;
  general purpose scissors for cutting through cords, braids and paper.
* Marking pencil: a tailor's chalk pencil, an air-vanishing pencil or one which can be erased with a damp cloth.
* Ruler and pencil.
* Bodkin or ribbon threader.
* Knitting needle.
* Fabric adhesive.

In addition to this basic sewing basket equipment, a sewing machine is essential for making up cushion covers. It will give a strong seam and will help to speed up the finishing process. Your sewing machine need not be elaborate. Apart from needing it to sew in a good straight line, there are just two basic requirements: a swing needle for zigzag stitching for finishing seams, and a zipper foot for attaching piping and zips.

A steam iron, or a dry iron and damp cloth, a pressing cloth and an ironing board are also essential for achieving good, neat results.

When you want a fresh look in a room, but don't want to re-decorate or buy new furniture, cushions in carefully chosen fabrics can add style and comfort. Only very basic sewing skills and equipment are needed to achieve stunning results.

Stitches

HAND SEWING

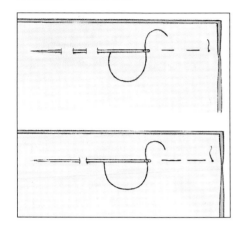

Tacking

Tacking is used to hold together two or more fabric layers temporarily, usually before machine stitching. Use tacking stitches of even length, about 6mm (¼in) apart, on areas that require more control, such as curves. Use uneven tacking for long straight edges, hems and trims.

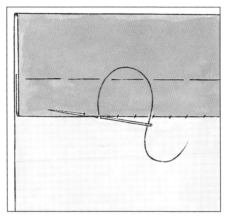

Hemming stitch

This is used to secure hems, for finishing the underside of a bound edge, and for appliquéing shapes to a base fabric. Fold under the turning, pin and tack it in place. Working from right to left, take a tiny stitch in the fabric and, without pulling the thread through, take a small stitch through the fold. Pull the thread through. Insert the needle in the main fabric below the first stitch and repeat, spacing the stitches about 6mm (¼in) apart.

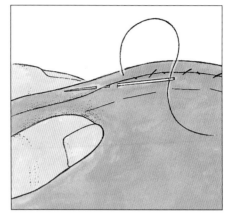

Slipstitch

This stitch is used to join two folded edges together, such as the closure on a simple cushion cover. Working from right to left, bring out the thread through one folded edge. Slip the needle through the fold of the opposite edge, for about 6mm (¼in), and bring out the needle. Repeat on the opposite side and continue in this way to the end of the seam.

MACHINE SEWING

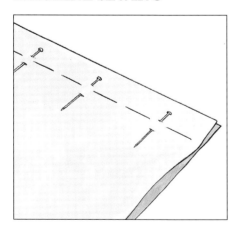

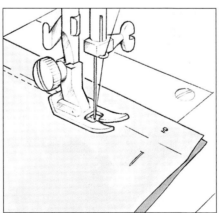

Plain seam

Most cushion covers require only a plain seam, which may be straight, curved or cornered. See page 43 for using the zipper foot for piped seams.

1 For a plain seam, pin and tack together the two pieces of fabric, right sides facing and raw edges even. Tack just inside the seam line.

2 Adjust stitch length to suit the cushion fabric, and stitch following the seam line. Remove tacking and press seam open on the wrong side.

Zigzag stitch

If your machine has a swing needle, use a medium stitch for neatening seam allowances on fabrics that fray easily, and a closer, wider stitch for neatening both seam allowances together.

Using Patterns

Some people prefer to work with a paper pattern, even for the most basic rectangular cushion covers, while others are happy to work with an outline drawn directly on to the wrong side of the fabric. However, a pattern is often necessary for unusual shapes.

The main benefit of a pattern is that it can be used again and again to cut fabric accurately to shape, with seam allowances included. It will also ensure that the fabric is cut on the required grain – one of the keys to achieving good results. All woven fabrics have a straight grain (this runs vertically with the warp threads) and a bias grain (this runs diagonally across the fabric).

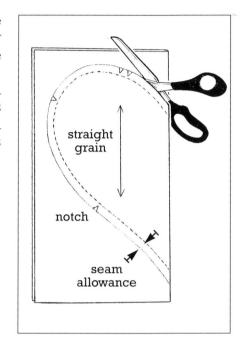

Symmetrical shapes

For symmetrical shapes, such as hearts, begin by folding a large sheet of paper in half lengthways and then drawing one half of the heart against the fold. Cut through both layers and open out the full heart-shaped pattern. Mark the straight grain parallel to the vertical centre line and cut one or two small notches (balance points) into the seam allowance. Make sure the notches match when joining two layers of fabric together.

Make rectangular and circular patterns in the same way, adding seam allowances, a vertical straight grain line and notches where required.

Enlarging a pattern

Some patterns given in the book need to be enlarged before being used to make paper patterns for cutting out fabric. By far the easiest way is to use a photocopier which can enlarge the image. If you don't have access to a photocopier you will need to use the grid method to alter the size of the pattern. The patterns on pages 25 and 59 are shown on grids with 1.25cm (½in) squares. If you want the finished pattern to be four times the size shown, you will need to draw a grid four times the size, ie with 5cm (2in) squares. It is easiest to draw this grid on graph paper.

1 Decide how big you want your pattern to be. Draw a grid, enlarging the squares by the required amount. In this example, the pattern is to be doubled in size so the large squares (right) are twice the size of the ones above.

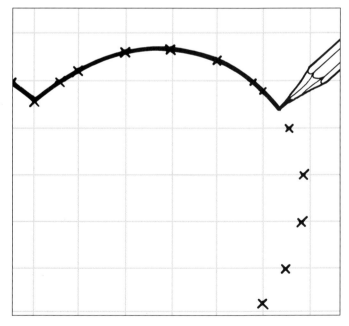

2 Lightly sketch the pattern on to the large grid, then copy the points where the pattern intersects the small grid. Use a ruler to join straight lines and copy the curves freehand. Transfer any instructions on the pattern.

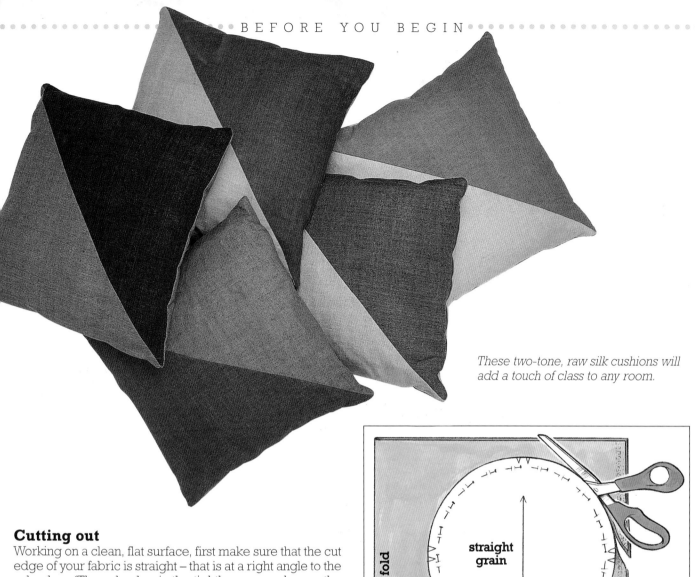

These two-tone, raw silk cushions will add a touch of class to any room.

Cutting out

Working on a clean, flat surface, first make sure that the cut edge of your fabric is straight – that is at a right angle to the selvedge. (The selvedge is the tightly woven edge on the lengthwise sides of the fabric.) To cut out a back and a front from plain fabric, fold the fabric with right sides together, place the paper pattern on the straight grain, close to the fabric edge (to be economical) and pin inside the seam allowance. Cut out using dressmaker's shears. On patterned fabrics with prominent motifs, open the fabric to a single layer, right side facing, and place your paper pattern over the appropriate motif. Pin, cut out and repeat for the second side as required.

Pressing

In pressing, a hot steam iron is placed on the fabric briefly, and then lifted off and replaced in short bursts. This technique is used to shape or smooth the fabric during the making-up process. For best results, pressing should be done at all stages of making up the cushions. If you do not have a steam iron, use a dry iron and a damp cloth. Where possible, press on the wrong side of a fabric. To press a plain seam, follow these instructions:

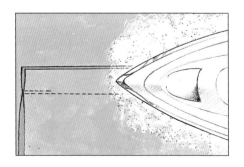

1 After stitching, remove the tacking threads and press the seam flat to sink the stitches into the fabric.

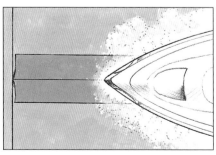

2 Press the seam allowances open. Also press the point of the iron under the raw edges of the seam to remove any marks which may show on the right side.

Simple Shapes

Square Cushion

The cover for a simple square cushion consists of a top and a bottom section. The cover should be about 2.5cm (1in) smaller than the pad to give a snug fit. Measure the pad from one side seam to the other, add a 1.5cm (⅝in) seam allowance to all sides and deduct the 'snug fit' allowance from each dimension to give the finished size of the cushion. An opening is left in one seam for inserting the pad and this is closed with slipstitches. If you want a different form of closure or decorative edges, it is important to read the relevant instructions before cutting your fabric.

You will need
Fabric
Square cushion pad
Basic equipment (see page 14)

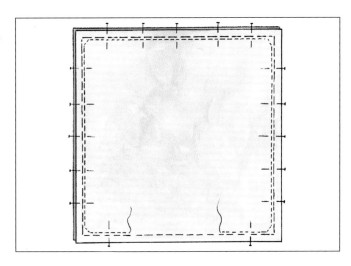

1 Cut out the front and back sections. Put them right sides together and pin and tack around all sides. Stitch on the seam line and across the corners (for a few stitches) to blunt them. Leave a central opening in one side.

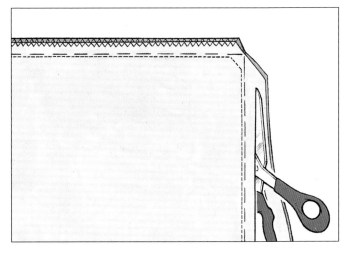

2 Trim across the corners to reduce bulk and neaten the seams. On fabrics that fray, trim the seam allowances and zigzag stitch close to the edge.

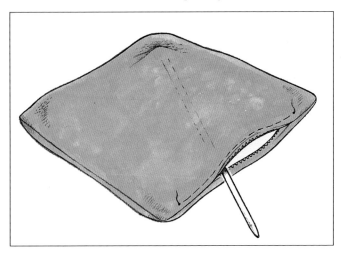

3 Remove the tacking stitches. Turn the cover through to the right side and ease the corners out using the blunt end of a knitting needle. Press the cover if necessary. Insert the cushion pad. Turn under the seam allowances on the open edges and tack.

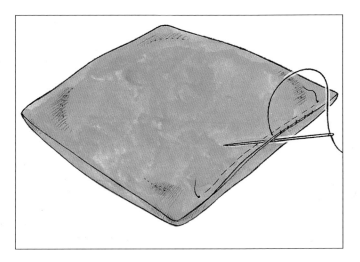

4 Using matching sewing thread, slipstitch the opening closed. Remove the tacking stitches and shake the cushion to distribute the filling evenly.

VARIATIONS

Variations to the square cushion include all rectangular shapes and a simple triangle, made by diagonally dividing a square. Make rectangular cushions in the same way as the square one, placing the opening along one long edge. The effect can be varied further by using contrasting coloured fabrics of the same weight for the back and front sections.

All square and rectangular cushions should be made with tight-fitting covers so remember to deduct the 'snug fit' allowance.

Triangular cushion

1 For triangular cushions (based on a square), begin by smoothing a square pad of the appropriate size diagonally across. Pin a line through both layers and shake the filling away from it. Tack and stitch. Repeat a second line 12mm (½in) apart. Cut through the middle and zigzag stitch to neaten the edges together.

2 Before cutting out your fabric, make a paper pattern based on the measurements of the square pad, allowing for deductions for snug fit as for the square cushion. Mark the straight grain and cut the paper pattern diagonally in half. Pin to your fabric, adding seam allowances on all edges, and cut out.

3 Make up the cushion cover as for the square cushion, making the opening in the long edge. Insert the triangular pad, then tack and slipstitch the opening closed.

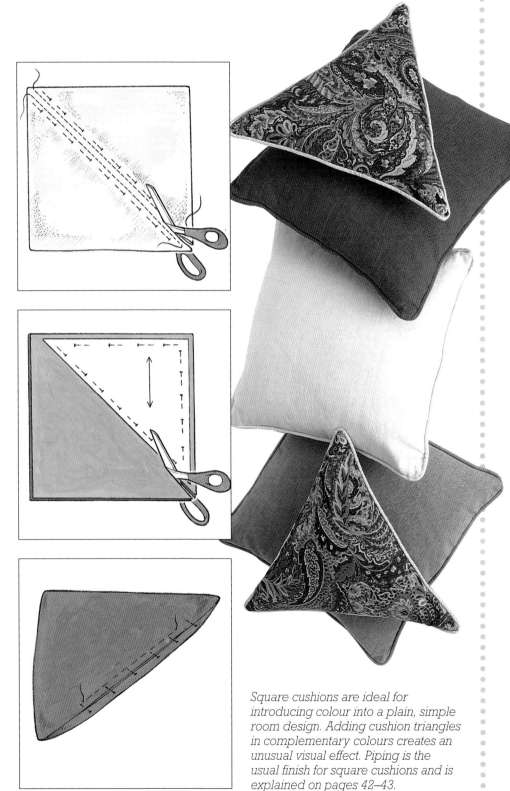

Square cushions are ideal for introducing colour into a plain, simple room design. Adding cushion triangles in complementary colours creates an unusual visual effect. Piping is the usual finish for square cushions and is explained on pages 42–43.

Round Cushion

Round cushion covers are usually piped or given a frilled edge to strengthen the seam. They can also be finished on the outside edge with cord or fringing. For decorative edgings see pages 40–49 before you cut your fabric. For a round cushion cover with a hand-stitched opening, measure the diameter of the cushion pad, add 3cm (1¼in) for seams and deduct 2.5cm (1in) for a snug fit.

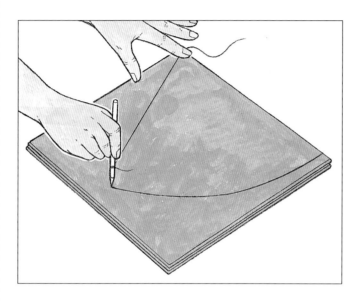

1 Cut a square of brown paper very slightly bigger than the measurement you have calculated from the pad and fold it in four. Tie the string around the pencil and, holding the string in the corner of the folded paper, draw a quarter circle to fill the paper. Cut around the line.

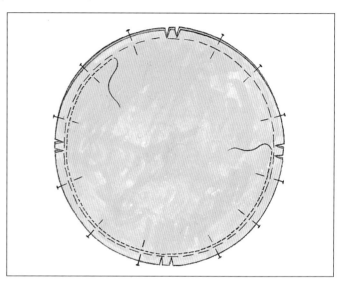

2 Open out the pattern and use it to cut out two pieces of fabric. Mark balance points (notches) as shown. With right sides facing, pin, tack, and stitch around fabric circles, leaving an opening of about one third of the circumference.

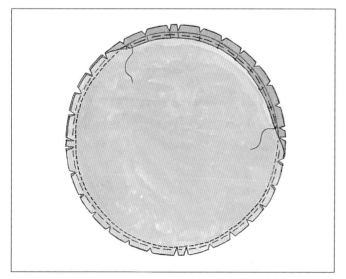

3 Remove tacking. Trim back the seam allowance to 12mm (½in) and notch at 4cm (1½in) intervals. Turn back the seam allowances on the open edges and tack.

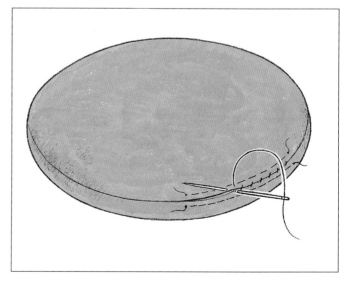

4 Turn through to the right side and press. Insert the cushion pad. Slipstitch the opening closed.

VARIATIONS

A fun variation on the plain round cushion is the half circle. You can use the same pattern and cut it in half, or make a bigger or smaller shape as you wish. A towelling half circle is ideal for cushioning your head as you lie back in the bath. Luxury half circles made in silk or velvet look wonderful with tassels (see page 48) on the bottom corners.

NOTE
Square box-sided cushion covers can be made in the same way as round ones, but the seams of the box-side are aligned with the four corners. For a zip closure, inserted into the box-side, see page 35.

Round cushions are best finished with piping or a frill. Otherwise it is very difficult to make a smooth edge.

Round box-sided cushion

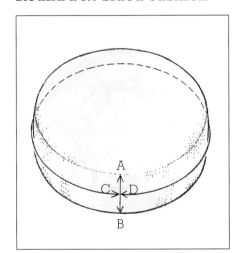

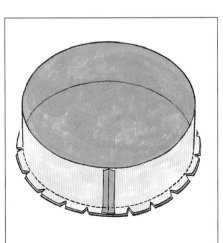

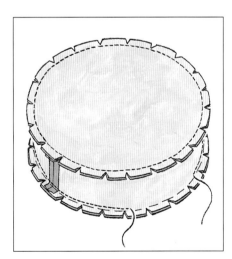

1 For a box-sided cover with a hand-stitched opening, begin by making a paper pattern for the top and bottom sections as for the plain round cover. Then measure the depth (A-B) and circumference of the pad (C-D), add seam allowance to all sides and make a pattern for the side piece.

2 Cut out the fabric pieces using the patterns. Right sides facing, join together the short edges of the side piece and press open. Notch the seam allowances of the top and bottom sections. With right sides facing, tack and stitch the side piece to the top circular piece.

3 Attach the bottom circular piece in the same way, leaving a third of the seam open. Fold over and tack the open edges. Turn the cover to the right side and insert the pad. Tack then slipstitch the opening closed. Remove the tacking stitches. Press.

Heart-shaped Cushion

On special occasions such as weddings and St Valentine's Day, heart-shaped cushions make an unusual and thoughtful gift. Small heart-shaped cushions can be filled with lavender or pot pourri and used to scent rooms and drawers. A heart-shaped sleep pillow, filled with herbs to promote a good night's rest, is an attractive addition to a pile of cushions arranged on a bed.

As heart-shaped cushion pads are not always available, you may need to make the pad as well as the cover.

| **You will need** |
| *For cushion pad* |
| **Casing fabric** |
| **Synthetic stuffing** |
| **Sheet of paper** |
| Basic equipment (see page 14) |
| |
| *For cushion cover* |
| **Fabric** |
| Basic equipment (see page 14) |

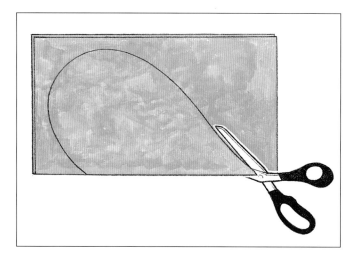

1 Cut a piece of paper a little bigger than the required size: 36cm x 33cm (14in x 13in) is an average cushion shape. Fold the paper lengthways in half and draw one half of a heart against the fold. Cut along the line through both layers, and open out the pattern (see page 16).

2 Using the pattern, and adding a 1.5cm (⅝in) seam allowance all round, cut out two pieces from the casing fabric. Make up following the instructions for the round cushion. Leave a 13cm (5in) opening in one seam. Stitch, trim and notch the seam allowances and turn through.

3 Turn under the seam allowance on the open edges and tack. Fill evenly with teased-out stuffing. Slipstitch the opening closed.

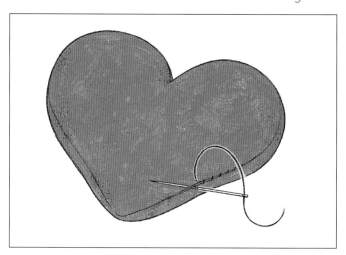

4 Cut out the cover using the pattern, but do not add extra fabric for seam allowances. This will ensure a snug fit. Make up following the instructions for the round cover.

VARIATIONS

The shape of the heart can be varied to suit individual tastes and the intended purpose of the cushion. The grids below give two alternative heart shapes which you can enlarge to the size you want (see page 16). Make a paper pattern and make up the cushion pad and cover following the instructions given opposite. For piped or frilled edges, see pages 40–43. For details of how to appliqué a motif to your heart pillow, see page 54.

Sleep pillow

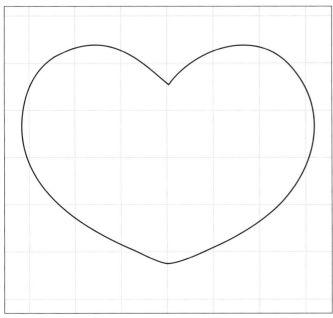

Wedding pillow

Colourful tartan and red hearts make a splash for Valentine's Day. Choose white lacy fabrics for wedding hearts. Small prints suit a sleep pillow or sachet.

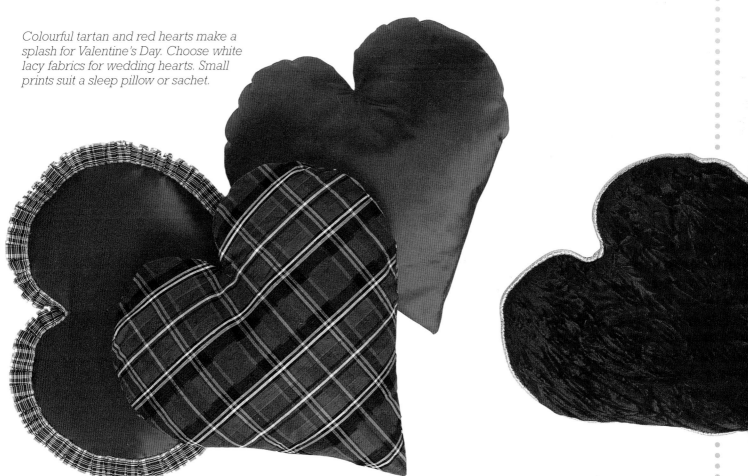

Bolsters

Traditionally, long, round bolster cushions are used at the ends of a sofa and at a bedhead. Bolster pads in different sizes are widely available and are usually firm, not soft and squashy like the typical round and square cushion pads. This means the cover needs to be cut to give an exact, tailored fit. A simple cover with flat or tied ends is quick and easy to make and looks very stylish.

You will need
Fabric
Bolster pad
Basic equipment (see page 14)
Paper for the pattern
Ties, buttons or tassels to finish

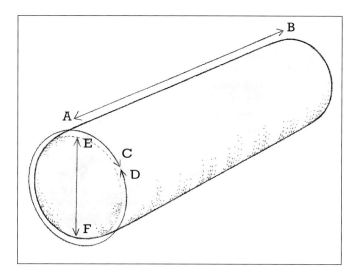

1 Measure the length of the pad (A-B) and the circumference (C-D). Add seam allowances and cut out fabric to size. Measure the diameter of the end of the bolster (E-F) and add a seam allowance. Make a paper pattern following the instructions for the round cushion (see page 22). Use the pattern to cut two round pieces of fabric.

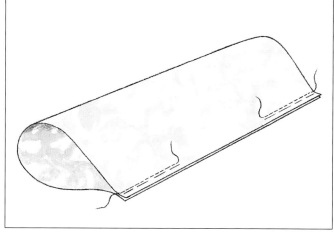

2 With right sides facing, fold the main fabric section lengthways in half. Tack and stitch across the long end. Leave a central opening about half the length of the bolster, for turning through and inserting the pad.

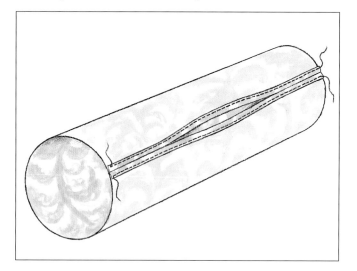

3 Press the seam open, neaten the edges by turning under 6mm (¼in) on each side and machine stitch. Notch the seam allowances of the two end pieces.

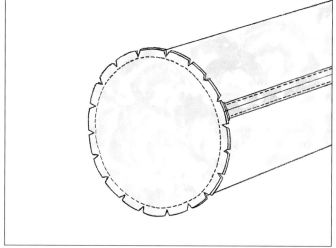

4 With right sides together, pin, tack and stitch the end pieces in place. Remove the tacking stitches. Turn the cover through to the right side, press and insert the bolster pad. Slipstitch the opening closed.

VARIATIONS

The ends of a bolster can be varied in several ways: they can be gathered into the centre and finished with a capping tassel or a large covered button or, instead of inserting separate ends, the bolster cover can be extended and tied decoratively rather like a Christmas cracker.

Tied ends

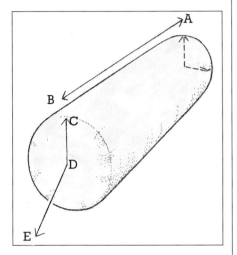

1 For tied ends, measure the length of the bolster pad (A-B) and, at both ends, add the radius of the end (C-D) plus about 20cm (8in) extra (D-E). Measure the circumference of the pad, add seam allowances and cut out fabric to size as bolster on page 26.

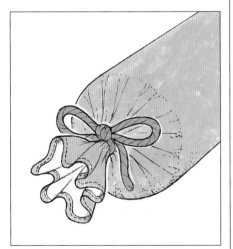

2 With right sides together, stitch the long seam of the bolster and press open. Make narrow double hems at each open end, stitch and press. Put in the bolster and tie the ends. Use cord or ribbon or make a matching fabric tie.

Gathered and buttoned ends

Measure around the circumference of the bolster pad (A-B) and the radius of the end (C-D). Cut two rectangular strips of fabric to this measurement, plus seam allowances. Make a cover as in steps 1,2 and 3 on page 26 but ignore instructions for the end pieces.

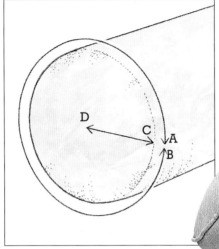

1 Stitch the two short edges of one end piece together. Press seam open. With right sides together, stitch to one end of the main bolster section. Make a single turning on the long edge and run two rows of gathering stitches around. Repeat on other end.

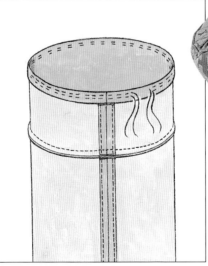

2 Pull up the gathers tightly, bringing the edges together to form a circle. Fasten off securely. Stitch a capping tassel to each end or cover two large button moulds with matching or contrasting fabric and stitch them over the gathered centre to finish.

Choose between tied, plain or gathered and buttoned ends for your bolster. Make bolster cushions to fit the ends of a sofa or make them giant-sized for a bedhead.

Bordered Covers

Giving a cushion cover a border, besides adding style and elegance, extends the size of the cushion. Big cushions with bold borders look good piled on beds and on large sofas and chairs. You can use matching or contrasting fabric for the cushion border, depending on your choice of method.

Self-bordered cushion

This border is made by extending the fabric of the front of the cushion to make a border front and back. The corners of the border are mitred on the back. The centre back of the cushion can be made in contrasting fabric.

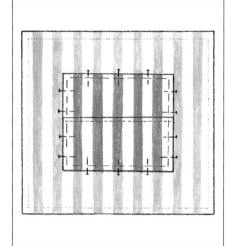

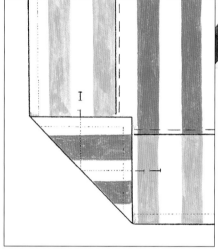

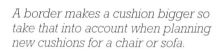

A border makes a cushion bigger so take that into account when planning new cushions for a chair or sofa.

1 To make a 8cm (3in) border, first measure the cushion pad both ways from one side seam to the other. Then deduct 2.5cm (1in) from the depth and the width for a snug fit. Add a 1.5cm (⅝in) seam allowance and twice the depth of the border on all sides. Cut out the front to these measurements. Cut out the back to allow for an overlapping closure (see page 32). Make up the back. With wrong sides inside, place the back and front sections together, pin and tack all sides, stitching just inside the seam allowance. Press a single turning on the raw edges of the border.

2 At each corner, mark the finished width of the border on both sides with pins, and fold over the corner so that the fold meets the marked point. Press then unfold the corners.

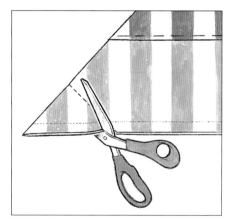

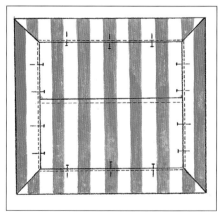

3 Fold the cover (with right sides of front together) diagonally through the corner. Tack and stitch along the crease up to the folded turning. Trim the seam to 1cm (⅜in), press open.

4 Repeat for each corner. Then turn each corner through, fold under the turning and tack in place. Machine stitch close to the edge, through all the layers.

You will need
Fabric
Square cushion pad
Basic equipment (see page 14)

Contrasting border

Cut out the back to allow for a central overlap (see page 32). Cut out the front cover following the instructions for a simple square cushion (see page 20). For the border, cut four side pieces the width of the cushion by the width of the border you want, plus seam allowances all round. Cut four pieces the combined depth of the cushion and both borders, plus seam allowances all round.

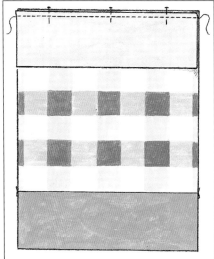

1 With right sides together, place the two shorter border pieces on the front cover with raw edges matching. Pin, tack if you wish, and stitch. Press the seams open.

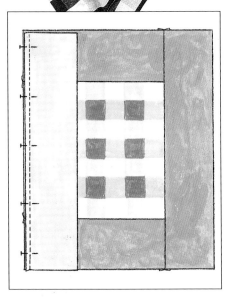

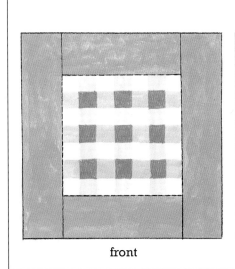

front

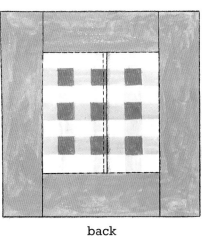

back

2 Attach the two longer pieces to the front and press. Prepare the back opening (see page 32), then attach the border sections in the same way.

3 Place the front and back pieces right sides together, pin, tack and stitch around all sides. Trim the corners, turn to the right side through the opening and press. Topstitch around the inside edge of the border through both layers, sinking the stitches through the previous stitching.

Fastenings
and Ties

◆

Overlapping Closures

To put the cushion pad into the cover, an opening must be created. An opening can be left in one of the seams and closed with slipstitches. However, if you need to remove the cover for cleaning, a central overlapping closure, fastened in some way, or an envelope closure is preferable.

Central overlap with touch and close fastening

A central overlap in the back of a cover allows the pad to be removed. It is created by making the back from two pieces of overlapping fabric. The overlap can be fastened in a variety of ways. Touch and close fastening consists of two strips of nylon tape, one covered with loops and the other with hooks. When pressed together these surfaces interlock firmly. Use this type of sew-in fastening wherever it will not be very visible or be put under great strain. It is fine for the back of a sofa cushion, for example. It is not recommended for fine fabrics such as silk.

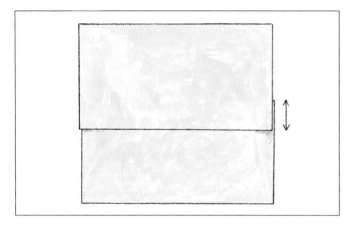

1 When cutting out the back section of the cushion cover, allow for it to be made in two parts so that the edges can be overlapped to form a central opening. To the dimensions of the pad, minus any deduction needed for a snug fit (see page 20), add seam allowances on all edges of both pieces and at least 4cm (1½in) overlap.

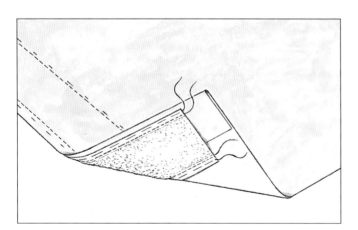

3 Sew the loop half to the underside of the overlap in the same way, having first made a single 1.5cm (½in) turning to the wrong side of the fabric.

2 Attach the touch and close fastening strips before the cushion cover is made up. On the underlap make a single 1.5cm (½in) turning to the right side and tack. Place the hook side of the fastening, right side up, close to the edge of the turning and tack in place. Using the zipper foot on your sewing machine, either straight stitch or zigzag stitch along both edges of the tape.

4 Make up the cushion cover with the opening closed. Place the front and back sections right sides together, pin, tack and machine stitch around, taking 1.5cm (¾in) seams. Trim across the corners, remove the tacking stitches and turn to the right side through the opening.

Buttoned overlap closure

A centre back overlapping closure fastened with buttons is both practical and decorative. Allow fabric for the two-part back section as for the touch and close fastening opposite, but increase the overlap to 10cm (4in) on each part to create a double 5cm (2in) turning. This will provide a strong base for the buttonholes. Attach the buttons and make the buttonholes before making the cover.

Plain envelope closure

This type of closure is made as an integral part of the cushion cover. The front of the cover is extended by about 15cm–20cm (6in–8in), folded back to form an envelope flap, and the side edges stitched into the seams. Envelope closures are particularly good for larger loose-fitting covers following a pillow-case style. On smaller covers, decorative ties can be used to close the flap (see page 36).

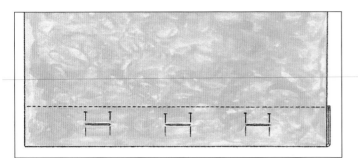

1 On both back sections, fold double turnings to the wrong side, pin and stitch across. Mark the positions and width of the buttonholes with pins, spacing them evenly across the overlap. If using a machine, follow the manufacturer's instructions for buttonholes. If working by hand, cut through the centre of each buttonhole.

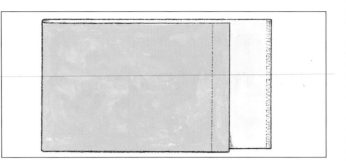

1 Measure the width and length of the cushion pad. Add 3cm (1¼in) seam allowances to the width. (No deduction need be made for fit since the cover is loose fitting.) Cut a single piece of fabric double the length of the pad plus 5cm (2in) for one turning and 18cm (7in) for the flap. Place one short edge on a selvedge.

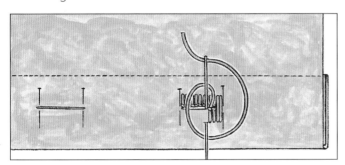

2 Using matching sewing thread, begin by making a line of running stitches around the cut edges. Working from right to left, bring the needle out through the slit and buttonhole stitch to the end. Make two stitches at the end and then complete the second side. Make two more stitches to finish.

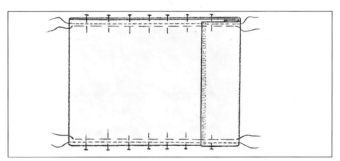

2 Make a hem on the short (raw) edge, turning in 12mm (½in) and then 5cm (2in) to the wrong side. Tack and machine stitch across. With the right sides together, fold the fabric widthways in half with the flap extended. Fold the flap over the hemmed edge, pin, tack, and stitch the side seams stitching through all layers.

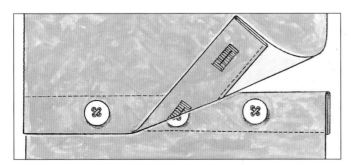

3 Overlap the two back sections. Mark the centre of each buttonhole with a pin. Using matching sewing thread, stitch the buttons in place, sewing neatly through all layers. Make up the cushion cover with the opening closed.

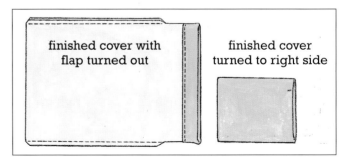

finished cover with flap turned out

finished cover turned to right side

3 Turn the flap right side out, and then remove the tacking stitches, trim across the corners and turn the cushion cover to the right side.

Zips and Press Studs

A zip is a neat and efficient way of closing a cushion cover. It can be inserted into a side seam or across the cushion back. Press studs are another quick and easy way of closing a cushion cover although they are not suited to delicate fabrics. They are best used to fasten a central back opening but can be used to close a side seam instead of slipstitches.

Zip in side seam

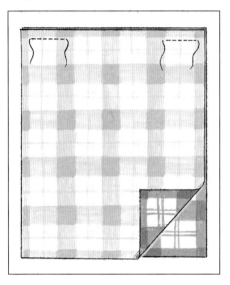

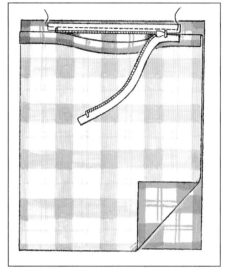

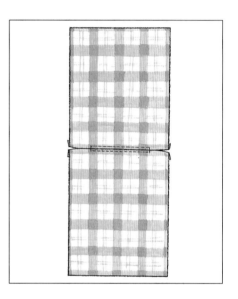

1 On the wrong side of the cover front, mark an opening the length of the zip. With the right sides inside, stitch the front and back sections together either side of the marks.

2 Open the zip and position one half face down on the seam allowance between the marks. Tack and, using the zipper foot, machine stitch in place, working close to the teeth.

3 Close the zip. Open out the cover, tack and stitch the other half of the zip to the back section, stitching across the ends to finish. Remove tacking and open the zip.

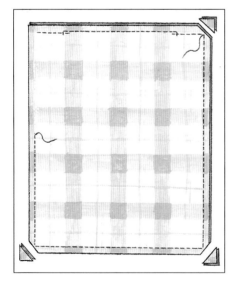

4 With right sides together, stitch around the remaining three sides. Trim across the corners and turn to the right side through the closure.

34

Zip in box-sided cushion

Follow the instructions on page 23, but make the side piece in two parts. The part for the zip should be about a quarter of the circumference. Cut this out, adding two seam allowances along the length and one at each end. Add seam allowances to the ends of the longer piece too. Cut the strip lengthways in half and insert the zip. You can put a zip in a rectangular box-sided cushion by making the opening the length of one side.

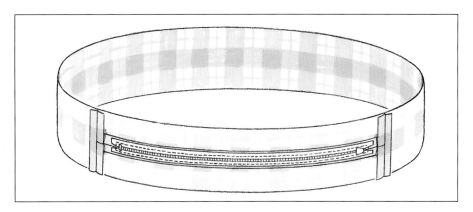

Press stud overlap closure

Press studs are available in several sizes and usually in either silver- or black-coloured metal. They are best used on a central overlapping opening and should be stitched in place before the cover is made up. Stitch them through the hems of the overlap for strength. Estimate the amount of fabric required for the cushion back as for the touch and close fastening (see page 32). Generally, larger studs are used on heavier fabrics. For very long openings, in big floor cushions for example, press stud tape is available.

If you want to put a zip across the back of a cushion, add an extra seam allowance to the top and bottom edges of the cushion back. Cut the fabric widthways in half and insert the zip as described opposite, before making up the cushion.

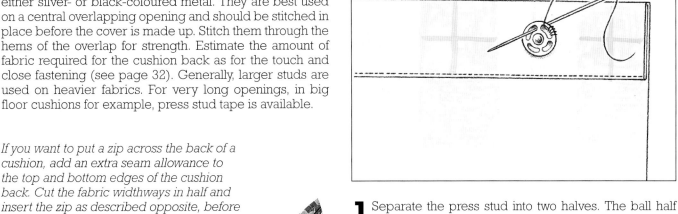

1 Separate the press stud into two halves. The ball half goes on the overlapping fabric; the socket half on the underlap. Position the ball half of the press stud on the wrong side of the overlap so that it is at least 6mm (¼in) from the fabric edge. Using matching sewing thread, make several small oversewing stitches through each hole, catching the hem only – so that the stitches will not be seen on the right side. Repeat for the remaining press studs, positioning them 8cm–10cm (3in–4in) apart.

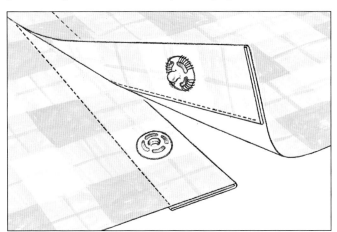

2 Overlap the two cushion back pieces and place them on a flat surface. Rub a little chalk on each ball and press them on to the underlap to mark the position for the socket halves. Sew these halves in place in the same way. Make up the cushion cover with the opening closed.

Tie Fastenings

Fabric ties, arranged as a pair of bows, can be a decorative feature in themselves. Ties can be positioned at the edge of the cushion cover to hold an envelope flap closed or they can be used to close an overlapping opening across the centre back of the cushion cover. In each case, the ties should be about 2.5cm (1in) wide and 30cm (12in) long. For each tie, measure the length plus 2cm (¾in) turnings at each end, and measure the width – 5cm (2in) plus 12mm (½in) seam allowances.

Basic tie

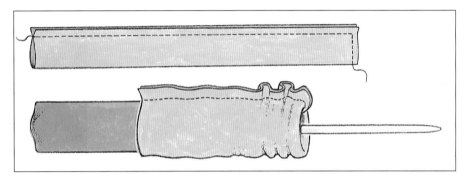

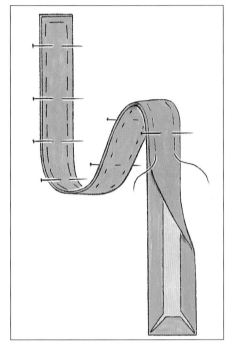

1 For medium-weight fabrics, fold the fabric lengthways in half, pin and machine stitch around two sides. Trim across the corners. Using the blunt end of a knitting needle placed in the seam at the short end of the tie,

turn the tie to the right side. Gradually ease the fabric over the end of the knitting needle as you push it through the fabric. Push out the corners and press the tie flat. Repeat for the remaining ties.

2 For heavy-weight fabrics, trim the corners of one short end, make single turnings along the two long sides and one short side. With the wrong sides together, fold the fabric lengthways in half. Pin, tack and press. Machine stitch around all sides close to the edge.

Tied envelope flap

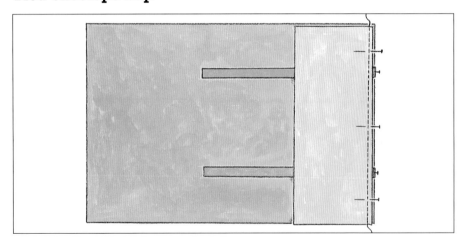

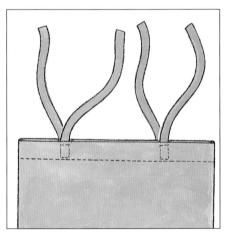

1 To attach ties to a cover with an envelope closure (see page 33), cut the flap separately, adding seam allowances. Before making up the cover, place the finished ties in position on the right side of the main

cover, raw edges even, and pin to hold. Then position the flap on top, right sides together, pin and stitch across. Press the seam and continue to make up the cover as for the envelope closure.

2 Attach corresponding ties to the hemmed edge of the cover, placing them on the inside of the hem. Make a single turning. Pin and machine stitch around to form a rectangle for strength.

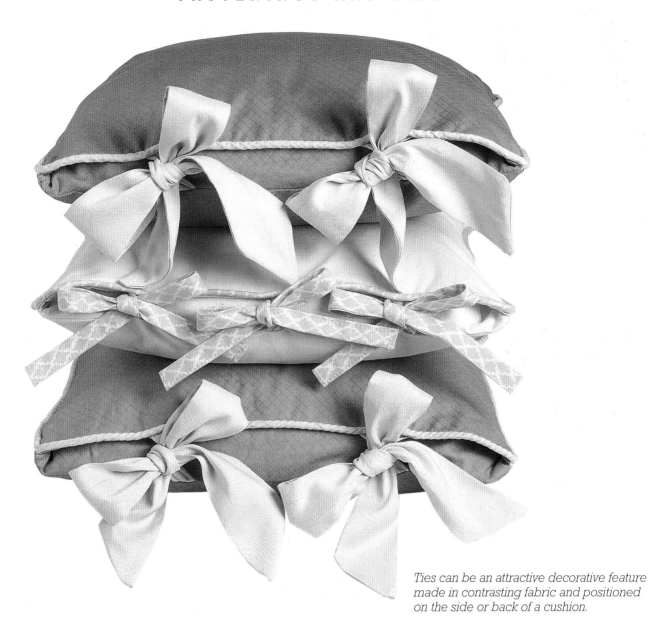

Ties can be an attractive decorative feature made in contrasting fabric and positioned on the side or back of a cushion.

Tied central overlapping closure

It is best to attach ties to a central overlapping closure before the cushion cover is made up. For cutting out the cushion back see page 32. Neaten the overlapping edge with a double turning and stitch across. Make a similar double turning on the under-lapped edge, folding it to the right side. Insert ties under the hem as shown in the diagram, tack and stitch across. Stitch corresponding ties to the wrong side of the overlap, first turning under the raw edge and then stitching through the hem to form a rectangle. With right sides facing, place the two sections in position and tack the overlapped edges. Join to the front of the cushion in the usual way.

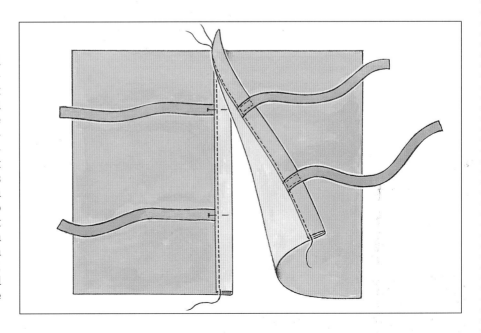

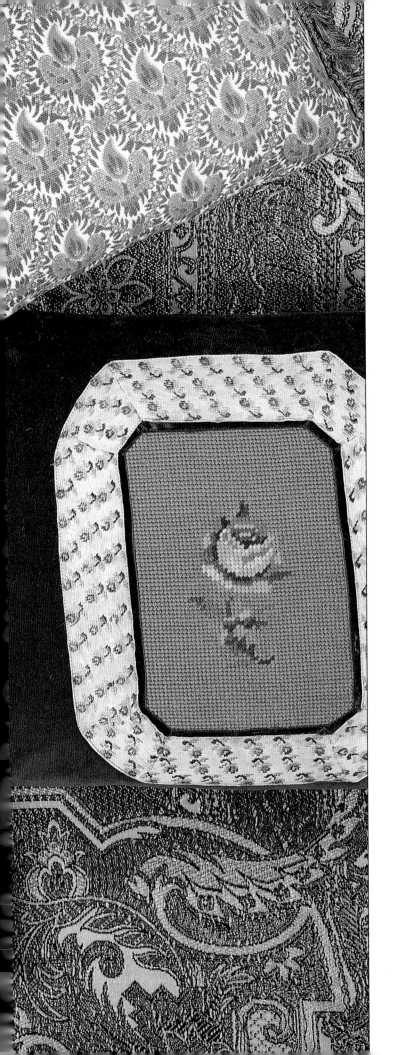

On the Edge

Frills

Pleated and frilled borders on cushions create a soft, luxurious look. They can be made in contrasting or matching fabric. Generally speaking, gathered frills are less formal than pleated frills and are ideal for bedrooms, garden chairs and cosy, informal settings. Pleated frills look great in rooms with heavy drapes and large, solid furniture. Some sewing machines have a time-saving attachment whereby fabric is pleated as it is fed through the machine. For hand pleating, careful measuring is needed.

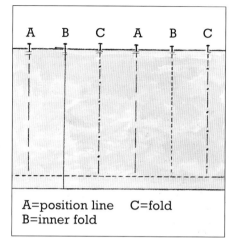

A=position line   C=fold
B=inner fold

Knife pleats

Decide on the width of pleat. Measure all around the edge of the cushion pad to get the overall length of the border. Divide this measurement by the width of the pleat you want to give the number of pleats. Multiply the fabric needed for each pleat (twice the pleat width) by the number of pleats. Add the length of border plus seam allowances for joining the ends. You will need a strip of fabric this long and as wide as you want your border plus seam allowances for joining to the cover. Cut and join fabric as necessary.

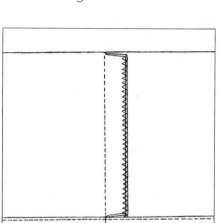
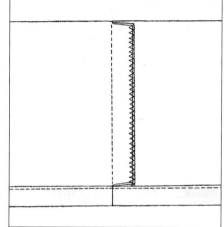

To combine piping and frills, first tack the piping to the cushion front, then tack the frill. Sew in place with one row of stitches.

1 If you have had to join fabric, press the seams to one side, trim and neaten. Neaten one long edge with a narrow hem.

2 On the opposite edge, use pins to mark off position and fold lines for the pleats. Work on the right side of the fabric. Place each fold line on its corresponding position line, and pin. Then tack just below and just above the seam line. Remove pins and press the pleats on both sides of the fabric.

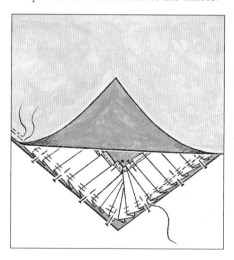

3 With right sides together, place the pleated border on the front cover, matching the raw edges. Pin and tack in place. At the corners, pin each pleat evenly. Take care to ensure the overlapping frill won't get caught in the stitching. Tack then stitch within the seam line. Pin and tack the back cover on top. Turn the cover over and machine stitch on the seam line. Leave a gap for turning, if needed. Trim corners and remove tacking before turning to the right side.

Frills suit a very feminine room and add a feeling of softness and comfort.

Gathered frill

Allow one and a half times the overall length of the border plus seam allowances for a gathered frill. When buying finer fabrics, such as broderie anglaise and lace edgings, allow slightly more for added fullness. The method for gathering the frill is the same whatever the type of fabric used. Ribbon can also be gathered in the same way.

1 Join any seams necessary to get a long enough piece of fabric for the frill, then hem one long edge as for the pleated border. Working on the right side of the opposite edge and using a long stitch, run two rows of gathering stitches just inside the seam line. Divide the frill into four and mark with pins.

2 With right sides together, attach the frill to the cover front at these points. Pull up the threads so that the frill fits the cover. Distribute the gathers evenly between the points marked, easing a little extra fullness around the corners. Pin at regular intervals and tack inside the seam line. Check the corners look neat. Machine stitch.

3 Pin and tack the cushion back on top, right sides together. Finish as for the pleated border.

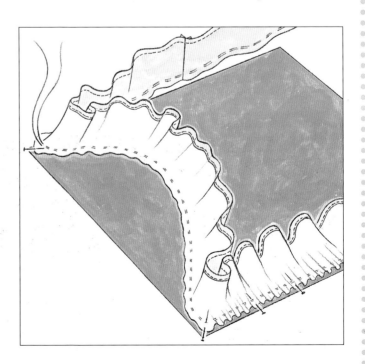

Piping

Corded piping gives an attractive finish to the seams of cushion covers. It consists of a pre-shrunk cotton cord covered with a bias-cut strip of fabric. Fold fabric at 45 degrees to the selvedge to cut bias strips. This gives the maximum stretch in woven materials. Alternatively, ready-made bias binding may be used. You may also find a range of ready-covered piping cords in larger stores. For making your own piping, cords are available in several widths but sizes 4 and 5 are generally used for home furnishings. To calculate how much cord is needed, measure around the cushion pad and add about 4cm (1½ in). Cut bias strips of fabric three times the circumference of the cord in width. Add 3cm (1¼ in) seam allowances to the length needed.

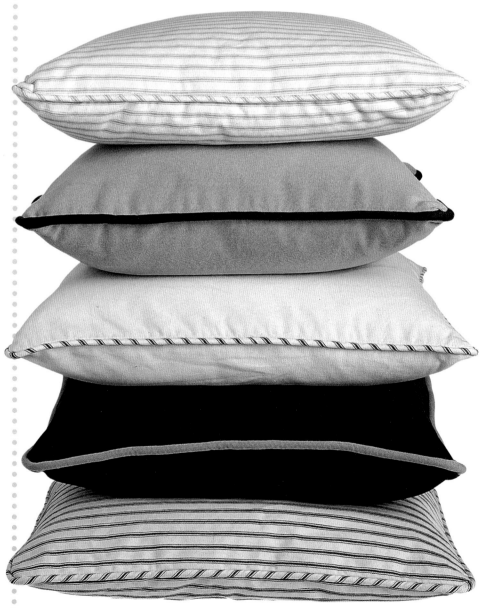

Corded piping

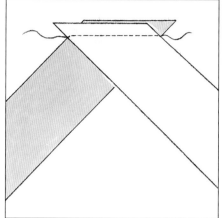

1 To make the required length, join the strips on the straight grain. Place the two strips right sides together, pin and machine stitch taking a 1.5cm (⅝ in) seam. Trim the seam to 1cm (⅜ in) and press open.

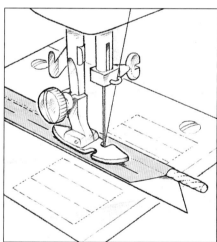

2 Fold the fabric strip around the piping cord, right side outside and raw edges even. Tack and stitch close to the cord, using the zipper foot.

Contrasting and matching piping both work well. If you are planning a number of cushions in a room, it is very effective to mix and match a range of contrasting fabrics.

Piping a seam

1 Position the piping on the right side of the cushion cover front, with the stitching on the seam line and raw edges matching. Tack in place about 3mm (⅛in) from the stitching. If the edge is curved, clip into the piping seam allowances to make them fit.

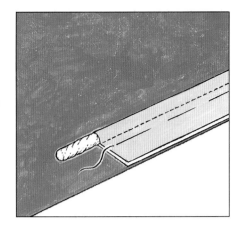

2 On corners, clip into the seam allowance almost to the stitching. Open out the piping to form a right angle, as shown. Pin and tack the piping in place.

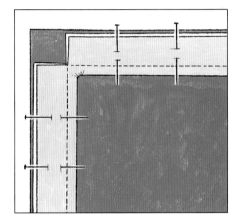

3 Using the zipper foot, stitch the piping in place working close to the first stitching. Press the stitching flat. If using a zip closure, the zip should be inserted before the back and front are stitched together. If you want both frills and piping, tack the piping in place first, then tack the frill on top before machine stitching through all layers.

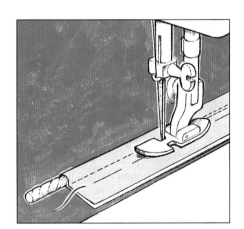

4 With right sides together, position the back section on top and tack in place. Turn the fabric over and, still using the zipper foot, stitch the seam, working between the previous stitching and the cord. Notch the main fabric seam allowances where the piping has been snipped, then turn the cover to the right side.

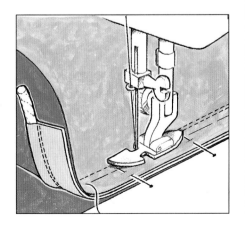

To join piping

Where a length of piping goes all the way around a cushion cover to the starting point, join the ends as follows:

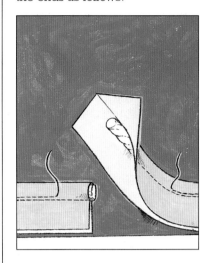

1 Position the piping so the join is on the bottom edge of the cushion cover. When stitching the piping to the cover, start 12mm (½in) from the end of the piping. At the other end, trim the cord to meet the first exactly, and trim the fabric so that it overlaps the cord by 12mm (½in).

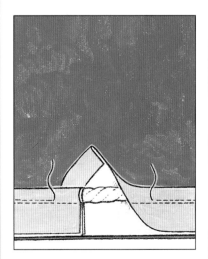

2 Fold under 6mm (¼in) of the trimmed fabric edge. Wrap the fold around the starting end as shown, allowing the cord ends to meet. Stitch across the join, extending it to 12mm (½in) beyond the starting point. Reverse the stitching to reinforce the join if needed.

Cords

Twisted cords are available in a wide variety of colours and thicknesses and may be used to trim the edges of a cushion – making an attractive alternative to piping. The least-conspicuous way to apply the cord is by slipstitching it by hand over the seam of the cushion cover. When stitching the cover, leave a 2cm (¾ in) gap in the seam for neatening the cord ends. Calculate how much cord is required by measuring around the cushion edge and adding 4cm (1½ in). Put a spot of glue on the ends of the cord before you start to stop them unravelling.

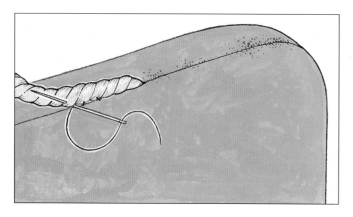

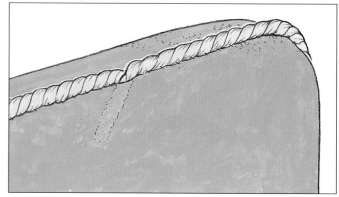

1 Insert one end of the cord into the seam opening. Working from right to left, take small stitches alternately through the underside of the cord and the fabric.

2 At the join, overlap the cord ends so that they cross each other smoothly. Secure with a few well-hidden stitches and close the seam in the same way.

The black cord provides a frame for the strong motifs of these cushions. It works well with the striped backing fabric too.

Braid and Ribbon

Braid and ribbon are best used for borders and bows and for covering seams and fabric edges. A huge range of colours and textures are available. Measure the area of the cushion to be covered and add a little extra for seams, mitring corners and neatening ends. As with other edgings, braid and ribbon are best added before the cushion is made up.

1 To apply a braid or ribbon border with mitred corners, begin by marking the braid width around the cover front with tacking. Pin and tack both edges of the braid, centring it within the marked lines. At the corners, fold the braid back on itself and stitch diagonally through all layers.

Ribbon has been used here for a gathered border and for decorative bows. The dimpling is achieved by sewing the bows on through the cushion and attaching a button to the other side.

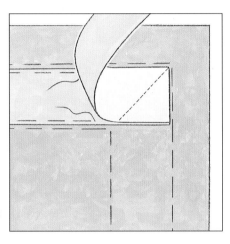 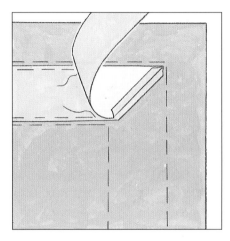

2 Trim away the fold, leaving a 6mm (¼in) seam and press open. Turn the braid to the right side and press the seam. Continue to pin and tack in this way until 10cm (4in) away from the starting point.

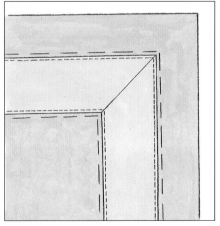

3 Press a diagonal fold at the corner, pin and stitch to the starting end, trim as before. Using matching thread, topstitch along both edges of the braid. Make up the cushion following your chosen method.

Fringes

Various styles of fringing are available for use on home furnishings. A wonderful range of colours and yarns including looped, tasselled, knotted and ball-edged fringes are widely available. Simple fringing can be made at home by fraying strips of fabric. This can be put into the seam line of the cushion and left plain or cut into shapes. Calculate the amount of fringing needed by measuring around the cushion pad and adding a little extra for each corner and seams.

Fringe with wide heading

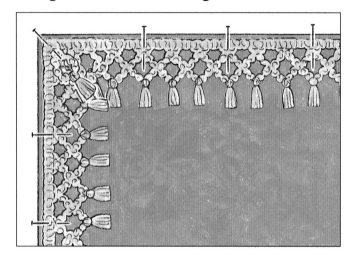

1 Fringes with a deep enough heading can be stitched into the seam of a cushion cover. Apply to the right side of the cover front and make up the cushion cover in the same way as the frilled cover (see page 40).

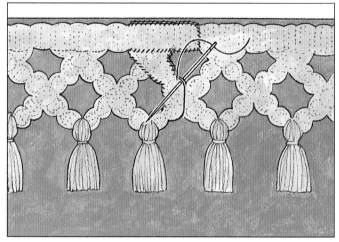

2 Join the cut ends of the fringe by overlapping them for about 2.5cm–4cm (1in–1½in), matching the pattern exactly. Position the join on the bottom edge of the cover. Using matching sewing thread, oversew the edges together. Trim the loose threads back to the stitching.

Fringe with narrow heading

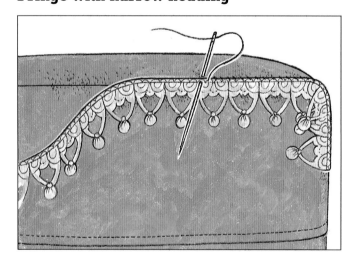

1 Fringes with narrower headings can be stitched to the outside of a cushion along the seam line. Working with the cushion back facing, position the edge of the fringe just over the seam line and pin in place. Ease a little extra fullness around the corners. Oversew the fringe to the front.

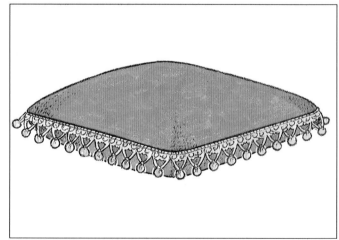

2 Overlap the cut ends of the fringe, match the pattern exactly and stitch the ends together, as for a wide-headed fringe. The fringe will hang down from the edge of the cushion to give a pretty effect.

Frayed fringes

Strips of fabric can be frayed and decoratively cut to make attractive, economical alternatives to purchased fringes. You can use the fabric from the main cushion, or select a contrasting fabric for your fringe. Decide the depth of the fringe you want: 4cm–6cm (1½in–2½in) works best. You will also need to add a 2cm (¾in) seam allowance.

Cut strips of evenly woven fabric to the length needed for your cushion and as wide as your chosen depth. Fray the fabric by gently pulling out the cross threads and teasing apart the remaining threads. Fray the threads up to the seam line on each fringe section.

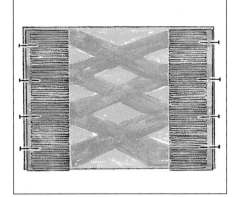

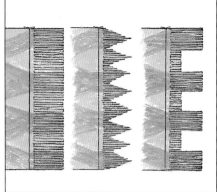

1 Pin and tack the fringe sections to the cushion front with the seam lines matching. Make up the cushion with an overlapping closure in the centre of the back (see page 32).

2 Turn the cover to the right side. Leave the frayed edges plain or cut out decorative shapes, measuring them with a ruler and marking with pins before cutting with sharp shears.

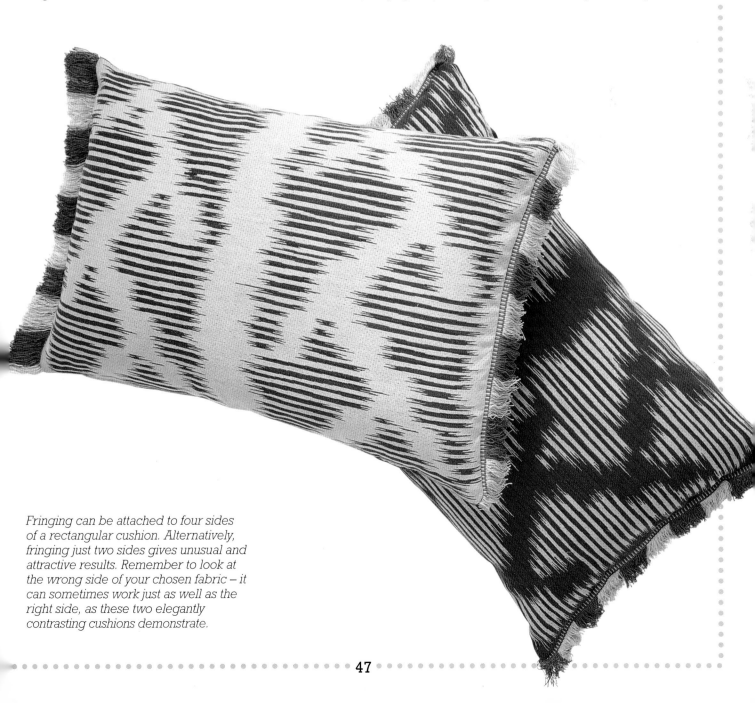

Fringing can be attached to four sides of a rectangular cushion. Alternatively, fringing just two sides gives unusual and attractive results. Remember to look at the wrong side of your chosen fabric – it can sometimes work just as well as the right side, as these two elegantly contrasting cushions demonstrate.

Tassels

Tassels make very attractive and elegant finishing touches and can be used on the corners or centres of cushions and at the ends of bolsters. Make them from yarn, cotton, silk, string or metal threads in plain or mixed colours, depending on the style and fabric of your cushion covers.

Simple tassel

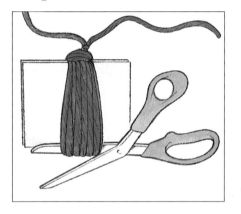

Large, silken fringes and tassels (right) are synonymous with rich and luxurious interiors. They look wonderful with strong-coloured, sumptuous upholstery.

Tassels (below) can also be used to pick up and accent contrasting colours in your interior design.

1 Cut two rectangles of stiff card the length of the tassel you want and about 8cm (3in) wide. Put the two cards together and wind the yarn around them 40–60 times. Thread a length of yarn on to a tapestry needle and pass it between the cards and under the strands several times. Tie the strands firmly together. Retain the yarn ends, which can be used to stitch the tassel on to the cushion. At the opposite end of the cards, cut through the strands and remove the cards.

2 Wind a length of yarn several times around the tassel 2cm–3cm (¾in–1¼in) from the tied end. Thread the yarn on to the needle and stitch through the binding to secure.

48

Simple tassel with cord

1 Buy or plait a cord and knot one end. Make a simple tassel as far as stage 1 (left). Open the strands of the tassel and thread the knotted end of the cord under the binding threads.

2 Fold the strands back again to cover the knot of the cord. Finish the tassel as in step 2 (left), winding a length of yarn around to make the top of the tassel.

Elaborate tassel

1 Using cotton or silk thread, make a simple tassel about 7cm (3in) long, with hanging cord, as described left. Make about 12 small simple tassels about 2.5cm (1in) long and retain the tying threads.

2 Attach the small tassels to the larger tassel. Stitch them through the binding threads. Leave a short length of thread so the tassels hang free. Stitch a row of beads to cover the main binding threads. Trim the tassel ends to finish.

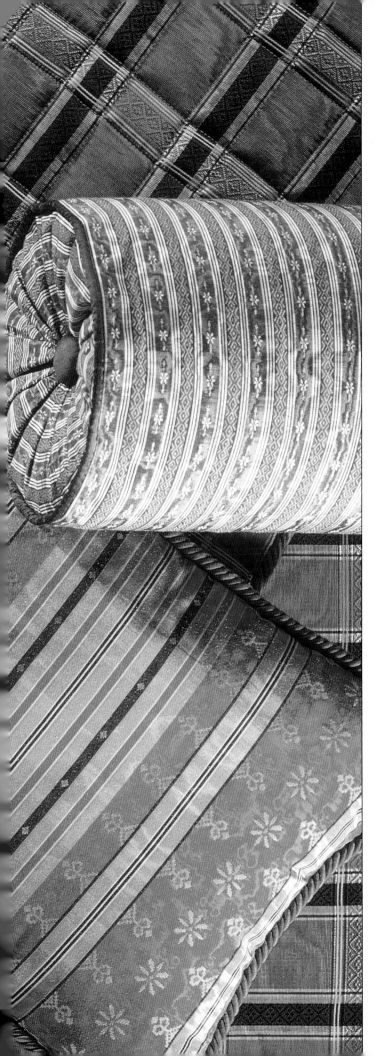

Special Effects

Buttons and Bows

The technique of buttoning, whereby pairs of buttons are attached to each side of loose cushions or fitted seating, is designed mainly to hold the filling in place. But they can be used decoratively to great effect. As the cover fabric cannot be removed easily once buttoned, choose a hard-wearing material. Bows are used in soft furnishings for all kinds of practical and decorative reasons. For a very special cushion, add a mock sash, tied in a huge, floppy bow, to a plain cover. The sash can be positioned across the centre or across one corner. Small bows, made of ribbon or fabric, look attractive sewn on to cushion corners.

Decorative buttons

Buttoning is done after the cushion is made. Buttons are sometimes added to sofa cushions, but usually they are found on fitted seating, where the cover is not removed. Thread can be used without buttons to create a dimpled effect, and this is called tufting.

Buttons covered in the same fabric as the cushion fabric look stylish. Contrasting fabric buttons will give an informal, fun look. Buttons can also be sewn on to cushions for a purely decorative effect.

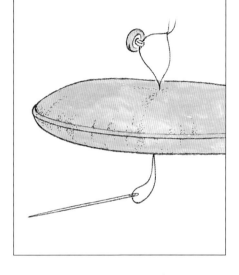 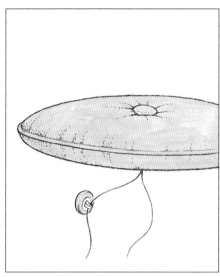

1 Thread a long needle with doubled thread. Tie the end of the thread to the button shank. Push the needle through the cushion.

2 Cut the thread to remove the needle. Tie on a second button. Tighten the knot to dimple the cushion and trim the ends.

Decorative bows

1 Decide on the type of closure for the cushion cover, estimate the fabric and cut out. For the sash, measure twice the width of the cushion pad by about 8cm (3in), plus 12mm (½in) seam allowances all round. Cut out four pieces of fabric to this size. For diagonally cut ends, place the four sash pieces together in pairs with the right sides inside and pin to hold. At one end of each pair, turn the corner over, as shown in the diagram, and crease the fold. Trim across, leaving a 12mm (½in) seam allowance.

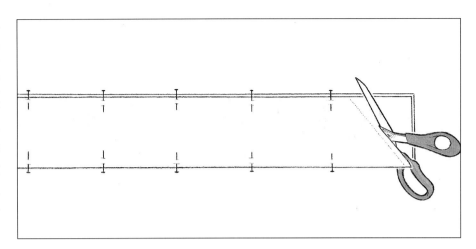

Fabric bows turn a simple cushion into a stunning talking point. You can even transform a square cushion into a round one by tying fabric bows around each corner and stitching them in place.

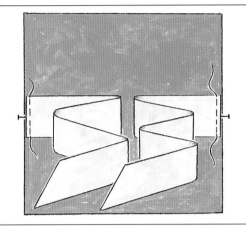

2 On each pair, machine stitch around three sides, leaving the short, straight side open. Trim across the corners, turn through to the right side and press under a cloth. Place the cushion front, right side up, on a flat surface and mark the centre of each side with pins. Lay the two sash pieces on the cover, centres matching, and raw edges even. Pin and tack within the seam allowance.

3 Make up the cushion and turn through to the right side. Lightly steam press, if needed. Insert the cushion pad, close the opening and tie the sash in a large bow across the front of the cushion to finish.

Appliqué

Appliqué is an excellent technique for utilizing fabric scraps. Contrasting motifs can be applied to a plain background either by hand or machine. You can cut out motifs using a paper template or cut around already-printed motifs. The raw edges of the motif are then turned in and hemmed by hand or tacked in place and zigzag stitched by machine. Appliqué offers the opportunity to pick a motif from your other soft furnishings – your curtain fabric for example – and use it on a group of co-ordinating cushion covers. For one-off, fun cushions, which make ideal gifts, cut out and appliqué appropriate motifs or letters. This underwater scene, for example, would look great on a bathroom chair or garden seat.

You will need
Cotton fabric for cover
Medium weight cotton fabric
for appliqué motifs
Cushion pad
Tracing paper and pencil
Embroidery threads
Sequins or small buttons
Basic equipment (see page 14)

1 Decide on the size and shape of the cushion you want and cut out the fabric for the front of the cover. Trace around the fish and starfish motifs on page 60 and cut out. Pin the paper patterns to the right side of your motif fabric and cut out as many motifs as you need for your cushion, adding a 6mm (¼in) seam allowance all round each motif. Remove the paper patterns.

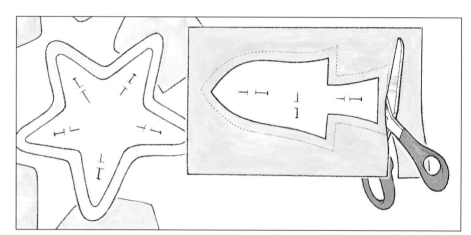

2 Arrange the fabric fish and starfish on the front of the cushion cover in a pleasing pattern. Snip into the angles on the motifs and notch the curved edges. With contrasting embroidery thread stitch the motifs in place using running stitches. Use the point of the needle to turn under the seam allowance as you sew. If the cushion will get heavy use, hem the motif in place with matching sewing thread before adding the decorative stitches.

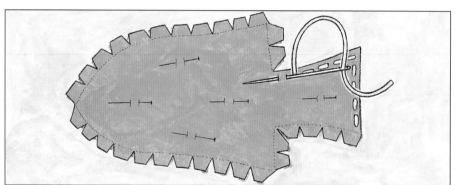

3 Attach a small button or sequin to each fish for its eye. Following the stitch diagrams opposite, add straight stitches to the fins and fly stitches for scales. Embroider clusters of french knots for the air bubbles leaving the fishes' mouths. When the front is finished, make up the cushion cover in the normal way.

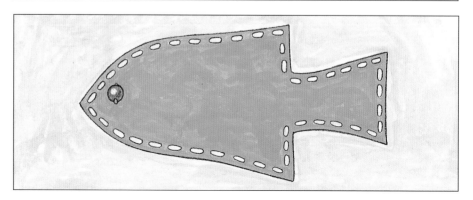

Stitching variations

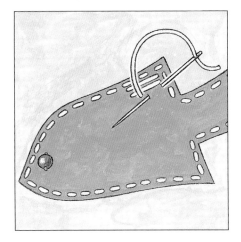

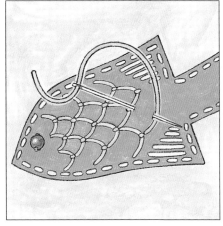

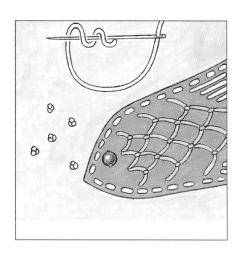

Straight stitch

Bring out the needle at the base of the fin, as shown in the diagram, take a straight stitch across and bring out the needle close to the starting point. Keeping to the inner contour of the fish, continue in this way to fill the fin. Work the tail in the same way, fanning the stitches to fill the shape.

Fly stitch

Bring out the needle at the top left and, holding the thread down with your left thumb, insert the needle to the right on the same level as the thread. Make a short downward stitch towards the middle and bring the needle out with the thread below. Insert the needle below the thread to make a short tying stitch and bring it out ready to work the next stitch.

French knots

Bring out the thread where the knot is to be worked. Holding it down with the left thumb, encircle it twice with the point of the needle. Twist the needle back to the starting point and insert it close to where the thread emerged. Pull the needle through to the back and repeat as needed.

One or two appliquéd cushions, matched with a group of plain cushions in contrasting and matching colours, will brighten up any room.

Patchwork

Patchwork uses pieces of fabric which are stitched together into a pleasing pattern, either by hand or by machine. Machine stitching is quick and gives a stronger seam than hand sewing. When planning your patchwork, it is best to choose fabrics of the same type and weight and to avoid very thick fabrics, which make it difficult to sew seams at the joins between the pieces. The simplest patchwork for a cushion cover front can be just four squares cut from two or more contrasting coloured fabrics. Two or four triangles also look very effective.

You will need
Fabric in two or more contrasting colours
Square cushion pad
Paper for patterns
Basic equipment (see page 14)

1 Measure the width and depth of the pad and deduct 2.5cm (1in) from each dimension for a snug fit. Cut out a square of paper this size. Fold the paper in half both ways, cut into four and mark the straight grain. Pin the paper patterns on the straight grain of the appropriate fabrics. Cut out the pieces, adding 1cm (⅜ in) seam allowances all round.

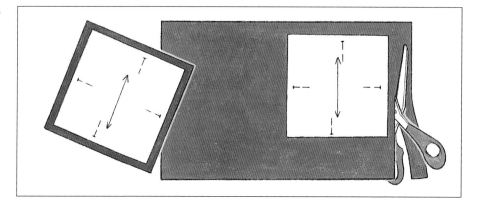

2 With right sides inside, pin one dark and one light square together. Machine stitch and repeat on the other two squares. Trim and press the seams open. On smaller patchwork pieces, the seams may all be pressed to one side for convenience and added strength.

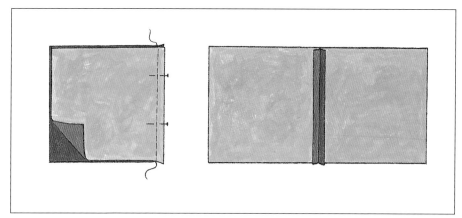

3 Place the two pieces of fabric in the correct chequered pattern. With right sides together, making sure the centre join is aligned, pin and stitch them across, carefully stitching over the pins. Trim and press the long seam open. Trim across the corners of the short seams in the centre of the cushion to reduce bulk.

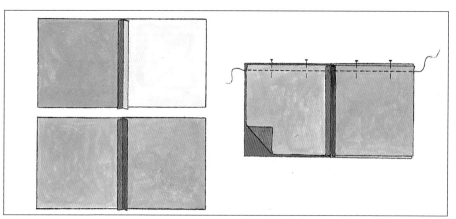

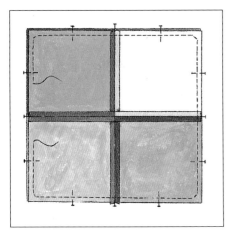

4 Cut out the back section, allowing for your chosen style of closure. Pipe the edges if desired (see page 42). Put front and back together and make up the cushion cover as normal.

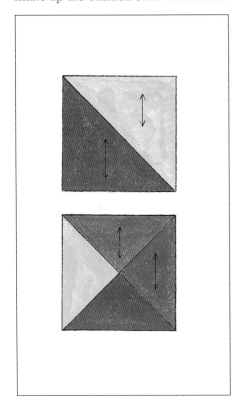

5 For two triangular patches, cut a square of paper, sized as for step 1 opposite, then cut it diagonally in half. For four triangular patches, cut the paper diagonally in half both ways. Continue as for square patches, being sure to add seam allowances.

A collection of cushions in matching and contrasting fabrics – some plain, some with patchwork squares and some with triangles – will make a stunning display on a plain sofa.

Quilting

Wadded quilting involves three layers of fabric – the top, a middle layer of wadding about 6mm (¼in) thick, and a backing layer. The layers are held together with lines of running stitches called quilting. Simple contour quilting is a relaxed style of quilting whereby a series of parallel lines are made around the outline of a motif, echoing outwards until they meet each other.

For a square cushion cover contour-quilted with a simple apple motif, quilt the cover top and make up as for the square cushion cover on page 20, with a slipstitched opening.

You will need
Cotton fabric for cushion cover
Synthetic wadding same size as front cover
Backing fabric same size as front cover
Cushion pad
Tracing paper and pencil
Basic equipment (see page 14)

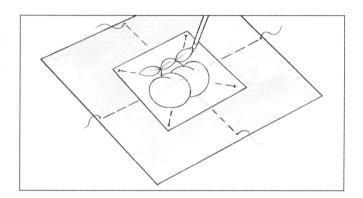

1 Mark the centre of the front cover fabric with tacking stitches. Trace the apple motif, enlarging it to a size to suit your cushion (see page 16). Position the tracing in the middle of your top fabric, centre lines matching, and pin to hold. Go over the outlines with an empty ballpoint pen. Work on a slightly padded surface so that the lines indent the fabric. You may prefer to go over these lines with an air-vanishing pencil.

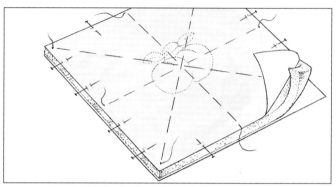

2 Assemble the three layers, cutting the wadding and backing fabric to the size of the cushion front. Put the backing right side down with the wadding on top, smoothing out any wrinkles. Then place the marked top cover right side up, with all edges even. Pin and tack together, stitching along both diagonals as well as vertically and horizontally.

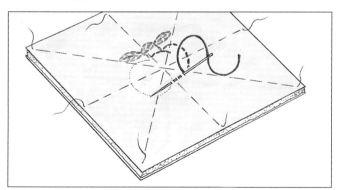

3 Thread a small quilting needle with red thread and knot the end. Pull out the thread at the top of the motif, bringing the knot through the backing and into the wadding. Quilt around the motif using small, even running stitches. Pick up three or four stitches on the needle each time before pulling it through. Outline the leaves with green running stitches.

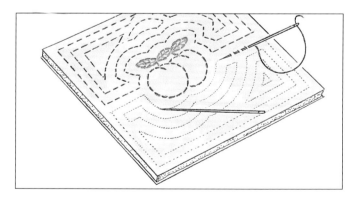

4 Place your quilting on a firm surface and, using the point of your needle, score the first contour line around the apples about 1cm (⅜in) away. This distance can be bigger or smaller, depending on your choice. Quilt in the same way and repeat more contour lines, breaking them where they meet others or the outer edge, to complete the design. Remove the tacking, except for the line around the edge, and make up the cushion.

Any simple design will look great when contour-quilted on plain fabric. Experiment with making the contour lines nearer together or further apart and try using different-coloured threads.

The apple motif will need to be enlarged and transferred to tracing paper before being used (see page 16). When enlarging the pattern, remember to leave plenty of room on the cushion cover around the motifs for the contour lines.

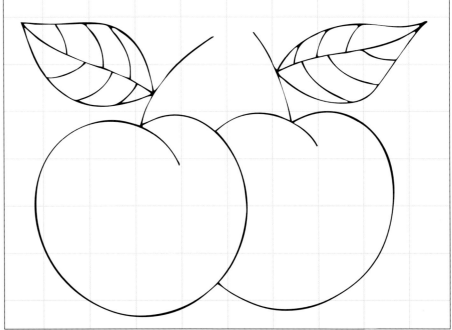

Templates

These two templates are used in the appliqué cushion on pages 54–55. They are shown here full size. If you want to use different motifs, choose shapes with simple, clear outlines. Purchased templates for alphabets are widely available.

Index

Acknowledgements

Most of the cushions photographed for this book were provided by:

Cushions
8 Impress House
Vale Grove
London W3 7QP
Telephone: 0181 932 8788. Fax: 0181 932 8790

We would like to thank Elizabeth, Nicolette and Roy at Cushions for all their help in making and choosing cushions for photography and Stof/SA for providing Cushions with the fabrics used for the covers on pages 12–13.

We would also like to thank the following who provided additional cushions and photographs:
page 10 Laura Ashley; page 11 (top) Grand Opera by Sanderson, page 11 (bottom left) Stof/SA, page 11 (bottom right) Next; page 14 Anna French Ltd from their Tapia collection; page 30–31 Annabel Claridge; page 38–39 Clare Callan (cushions from antique fabrics – telephone: 01747 852131); page 41 Ville de Lyon by Sanderson; page 45 Annabel Claridge; page 48–49 Osborne and Little plc from their Durbar Collection; page 50–51 Osborne and Little plc from their Durbar Collection; page 55 and page 59 cushions made by Gail Lawther.

Editor Katie Preston
Design Robert Mathias
Photography Andrew Sydenham
Step by step illustrations John Hutchinson